UNLEASH

YOUR

INNER POWER

Your Path to Personal Empowerment and Success

DR. JEFFERY ROYAL

CONTENTS

In the quiet town of Serenity Springs, a person like you and me lived. John, an ordinary individual with extraordinary dreams, stood at the crossroads of stagnation and potential. A victim of self-imposed limitations, John's journey is not just his own—it mirrors our struggles, aspirations, and untapped potential.

Once upon a time, John's days were overshadowed by the looming weight of doubt and fear. His dreams seemed galaxies away, and the path to success felt like an impossible maze. His internal dialogue whispered a tale of limitations, echoing the collective doubts that often hold us back from achieving our true potential.

As the sun set on another day filled with unrealized ambitions, John stood at the precipice of change. In that moment of reflection, he realized the power he held within—the ability to break free from the chains of limiting beliefs and forge a path towards personal success and empowerment.

In "Unleash Your Inner Power," we embark on a transformative journey inspired by stories like John's—stories that resonate with the deepest corners of our desires and aspirations. This book is not a mere guide but a companion on your expedition to overcome fears, silence self-doubt, and sculpt a life defined by your dreams.

Within these pages, you'll discover:

- Strategies to recognize and surmount your limitations.
- The scientific foundation of visualization and positive thinking.
- Techniques to establish and achieve personal goals.
- Productivity and time management hacks for daily success.
- The science behind habit development and techniques for positive change.
- Communication skills, resilience, and emotional intelligence strategies.
- Building a robust support system and fostering meaningful relationships.
- Insights into wealth creation, financial planning, and achieving financial security.
- Mindfulness and meditation practices for inner calm and peace.
- Motivational stories of individuals who turned adversity into triumph and a lot more.

Join us as we unravel the layers of your potential, just as John did. Together, we will navigate the intricacies of personal development, celebrating each triumph and embracing growth with open arms.

As you turn the pages of "Unleash Your Inner Power," remember that your story is waiting to be written. The journey begins now. Embrace it.

Personal limitations are sometimes regarded as internal limitations that prevent people from reaching their maximum potential. These limitations may appear in several forms, such as fear, self-doubt, limiting beliefs, and prior experiences. This section will examine the many forms of personal limitations and how they might influence us.

One of the most prevalent personal limits is fear. It may keep us from taking chances, doing new things, or following our dreams. Dread may manifest itself in various ways, including the dread of failure, rejection, and the unknown. For example, someone who is frightened of public speaking may shun chances to speak in public, even if they might enhance their career or personal development. Fear may also create a vicious cycle in which ignoring the fear reinforces and strengthens it.

Another form of personal limitation that might hold us back is self-doubt. The inner voice tells us we are not good, clever, or skilled enough to attain our goals. Past experiences or bad criticism from others might cause self-doubt. A lack of self-esteem or confidence may also cause it. Self-doubt may be deceptive, preventing us from taking risks and seizing chances. Limiting beliefs are deeply rooted attitudes or beliefs that keep us from moving forward. They might be conscious or unconscious, affected by our upbringing, society, and previous experiences.

Limiting beliefs may take various forms, such as "I am not smart enough to go to college" or "I don't have what it takes to start a business." These ideas might become self-fulfilling and inhibit us from taking action to attain our goals. Personal limitations might also stem from past experiences. Negative past experiences may lead to restrictive thoughts, anxiety, and self-doubt that impede us from going ahead. Someone who has been through a terrible occurrence, for example, may battle with anxiety and avoid circumstances that remind them of their trauma.

Personal limitations may have far-reaching consequences. They may keep us from reaching our goals, following our aspirations, and having a meaningful life. Personal limitations may sometimes lead to negative self-talk and a loss of confidence and self-esteem. Personal limitations may lead to emotions of dissatisfaction, helplessness, and pessimism over time. However, it is important to understand that personal limitations are not permanent. It is possible to overcome them with knowledge and the appropriate mentality. One method is to identify and confront the source of the limitation. For example, if fear of public speaking is restricted, one may begin by speaking in front of a small crowd and progressively increase the size of the audience.

Reframing negative self-talk into positive self-talk is another method. Negative ideas must be challenged and replaced with positive affirmations. Instead of thinking, "I am not good enough," consider, "I am capable and deserving of success."

Finally, personal limitations may manifest in various ways, including fear, self-doubt, limiting beliefs, and prior experiences. These limitations may greatly influence our lives, stopping us from reaching our goals and living a meaningful life. However, with awareness and the correct mentality, we may transcend our limitations and fully realize our potential. We may break free from the shackles of personal limitations and realize our aspirations by questioning negative beliefs, reframing self-talk, and making tiny efforts toward our goals.

How to recognize one's limits

Personal limitations may emerge in various aspects of our lives, including relationships, employment, health, and personal development. These limitations may prevent us from realizing our greatest potential, accomplishing our goals, and enjoying a meaningful life. As a result, it is critical to recognize and conquer them to unlock our inner potential and live our greatest life.

Here are some practical ways to identify your limitations:

Self-reflection is valuable for understanding one's thoughts, feelings, and actions. It may assist you in identifying behavioral patterns that may restrict your development and impede your success. Find a quiet and comfortable place, set aside some time, and think about your experiences, thoughts, and behaviors to practice self-reflection. "What are my strengths and weaknesses?" "What are my fears and doubts?" "What behavioral patterns do I see in myself?" and "What are my values and beliefs?" are some questions you might ask yourself.

Seek feedback from others: Sometimes, we may be ignorant of our limits, and obtaining feedback from others might help us acquire a new perspective. Request input from friends, family, coworkers, or mentors about your strengths and shortcomings, places for development, and chances for progress. Be receptive to constructive criticism and utilize it to help you learn and improve.

Analyze your previous experiences: Our past experiences can affect our views, attitudes, and actions. Analyzing your previous experiences helps you understand how they affected your present limitations. Consider the events that have influenced your views and values and the situations that have challenged and inspired you. Examine your lessons from these encounters and how you may apply them to your present circumstances.

Take personality and aptitude tests: Personality and aptitude tests may reveal important information about your skills, shortcomings, and potential. They may assist you in understanding your natural tendencies, preferences, and talents. To better understand yourself, take a personality test like Myers-Briggs or the Big Five Personality Traits or an aptitude exam like StrengthsFinder or Career Key.

Identify your limiting beliefs: These self-imposed ideas prevent us from realizing our greatest potential. They might include thoughts like "I'm not good enough," "I don't deserve success," or "I'm not smart enough." These views might result from previous experiences, cultural or social pressures, or self-doubt. Identify your limiting ideas and provide proof to the contrary. For example, if you feel you are not good enough, list the facts that refute this perception, such as your previous successes, talents, and positive comments from others.

The next stage is overcoming your own limitations after discovering them. Here are some tips to assist you overcome your limitations:

Set attainable goals: Setting attainable goals might assist you in breaking down your limitations into achievable stages. Set explicit, quantifiable, attainable, relevant, and time-bound goals concerning your values and vision. Divide your goals into smaller activities and rank them according to significance and urgency.

Develop a growth mentality: A growth mindset is the concept that our talents and intellect can be improved through hard effort and devotion. You may exceed your limits by accepting difficulties, learning from failure, and persevering in the face of adversity. Reframe your difficulties as chances for progress, and concentrate on the process rather than the end.

Take action: Taking action is important in overcoming your limits. It may assist you in developing confidence, gaining experience, and overcoming fear and self-doubt.

Fear is a natural feeling that all people experience, and it functions as a protective mechanism that assists us in avoiding danger. Fear, on the other hand, maybe crippling and hinder us from realizing our greatest potential. In this part, we'll talk about typical anxieties that hold us back and provide practical solutions to overcome them.

Fear of Failure

One of the most prevalent anxieties that prevents individuals from following their aspirations and taking chances is the fear of failing. It is the dread of failing and suffering the negative repercussions of failure, such as disappointment, humiliation, and disgrace. This dread might paralyze us and hinder us from taking action toward our goals. We must redefine our view on failure to overcome our fear of failure. Failure is a chance to learn, develop, and improve, not a reflection of our values or abilities. We may lessen the fear of failure by accepting it as a normal part of learning and approaching obstacles with a growth mentality. Another method for overcoming failure fears is to divide our ambitions into smaller, more manageable activities. This method helps us to concentrate on progress rather than perfection, allowing us to gain momentum toward our ultimate objective. It also aids in developing resilience and the ability to recover from setbacks.

Fear of Rejection

Fear of rejection is another prevalent worry that might prevent us from following our aspirations and building meaningful relationships. It is the dread of being hated, rejected, or outcast by others. This apprehension may result in self-doubt, poor self-esteem, and social anxiety. Recognizing rejection as a normal part of life is vital for overcoming rejection anxiety. It's acceptable if not everyone likes or agrees with us. We have no control over how people see us, but we influence how we react to rejection. We may decrease the effect of rejection on our self-esteem by creating a strong sense of self-worth and self-acceptance. Another method for overcoming rejection anxiety is to practice vulnerability. Vulnerability is the readiness to reveal ourselves and be open to comments and ideas from others. By embracing vulnerability, we may create stronger relationships with people and a higher feeling of empathy and understanding.

Fear of Change

Fear of change is a typical apprehension that might prevent us from seeking new chances and taking risks. It is the dread of the unknown and the uncertainty that it entails. This anxiety may result in complacency, stagnation, and lost opportunities. To overcome the fear of change, adopting a growth and adaptable attitude is critical. Change is unavoidable, and by embracing change, we may build the skills and resilience required to succeed in a world that is continuously changing.

Change may also be seen as a chance for personal development and self-discovery. Another method for overcoming fear of change is to divide the change into manageable stages. We may decrease the stress and anxiety associated with change by making tiny, gradual efforts toward it. To keep on track, we may also seek help from others and create a network of accountability.

Fear of Success

Although the fear of success is less widespread, it may prevent us from reaching our greatest potential. It is the dread of success's duties and expectations and the fear of being evaluated or blamed for our accomplishments. Fear of failure may result in self-sabotage, impostor syndrome, and wasted chances. We must rethink our view on success to overcome our fear of success. Success is not something to be afraid of or embarrassed by; it results from our hard work and devotion. We may boost our confidence and self-esteem by embracing success and celebrating our accomplishments.

Many individuals confront self-doubt and negative self-talk as obstacles on their personal development path. They may prevent you from following your dreams and reaching your full potential. There are, however, tactics that may be used to combat self-doubt and negative self-talk.

Recognize your self-talk tendencies: The first step is to become conscious of your self-talk tendencies to overcome self-doubt and negative self-talk. When confronted with a difficult scenario, pay attention to the concepts that arise in your head. Do you think more negatively or positively? Are your ideas reasonable or irrational? You may begin to confront and reframe your self-talk routines after identifying them.

Face your negative self-talk: Test your negative self-talk by asking yourself whether your ideas are sensible or irrational. When you see yourself spiraling into negative thinking, step back and attempt to look at the issue objectively. Ask yourself, "What evidence do I have that supports this thought?" and "Is there evidence that contradicts this thought?" You may break free from your negative self-talk by challenging its reality.

Reframe your inner dialogue: After you've questioned your negative self-talk, recast it more positively. Instead of concentrating on the issues, change your emphasis to the positives. Instead of thinking, "I'm not good enough," try, "I'm capable of overcoming this challenge." You may modify your

15

perception of yourself and your talents by reframing your self-talk.

Exercise self-compassion: Self-compassion is another approach to overcoming self-doubt and negative self-talk. Treat yourself with the same compassion and understanding you would provide to a close friend or loved one. Recognize your sentiments and remind yourself that everyone makes errors when they make a mistake or face a setback. By practicing self-compassion, you may strengthen your resilience and recover more quickly from setbacks.

Visualize your achievement: Visualizing success might help you overcome self-doubt and negative self-talk. Spend a few minutes each day visualizing yourself achieving your goals. Consider yourself conquering barriers, realizing your goals, and feeling proud of your achievements. Visualizing achievement might help you gain confidence and determination to pursue your goals.

Surround yourself with positive people: Another strategy to combat self-doubt and negative self-talk is to surround oneself with positive influences. Seek out supporting and encouraging friends, family members, and mentors. Avoid negative or criticizing individuals since they might drag you down and enhance your self-doubt. You may develop a support network to help you remain motivated and on track by surrounding yourself with good influences.

Celebrate your accomplishments: Finally, recognize them, no matter how little they may be. Recognize your accomplishments and credit yourself for your hard work and devotion. Celebrating your accomplishments might help you gain confidence and keep track of your development. It might also assist you in being motivated and focused on your goals.

Finally, self-doubt and negative self-talk might prevent you from reaching your greatest potential. You may overcome self-doubt and accomplish your goals by understanding your self-talk patterns, questioning your negative self-talk, reframing your self-talk, practicing self-compassion, envisioning achievement, surrounding yourself with positive influences, and celebrating your triumphs. Remember that self-improvement is a process that requires time and effort. You may, however, unlock your inner force and reach your maximum potential with dedication and a development mentality.

TECHNIQUES FOR OVERCOMING LIMITING BELIEFS

Limiting beliefs are deeply embedded mental patterns that impede our development and progress toward our goals.

These beliefs are formed due to previous experiences, societal training, and self-doubt, and they may keep us from realizing our greatest potential. To overcome these limiting ideas, we must first recognize them and then replace them with more powerful ones.

Here are some techniques for overcoming limiting beliefs:

Recognize and challenge your limiting beliefs:
Recognizing limiting beliefs is the first step in overcoming them. This necessitates being conscious of your thinking patterns and being honest with yourself about the ideas holding you back. Write down any beliefs that are keeping you from attaining your goals. This helps you gain clarity and perspective on what needs to be changed.

Challenge your limiting beliefs: Now that you've discovered your limiting beliefs, it's time to put them to the test. Consider if your opinions are founded on facts or assumptions. Many limiting beliefs are the result of incorrect assumptions and negative self-talk. By confronting these ideas, you may begin to replace them with more positive and powerful ones.

Reframe your beliefs: Reframing is a strong method that includes shifting your perspective on a circumstance or idea. Instead of seeing a limitation as a disadvantage, consider it an opportunity for development and learning. Instead of thinking, "I can't do this," rephrase it as "I don't know how to do this yet, but I am willing to learn."

Use positive affirmations: Affirmations are an excellent approach to replace limiting beliefs with empowered ones. Make a list of positive affirmations confirming your goals and skills, and repeat them to yourself daily. In other words, "I am capable of achieving my goals" and "I am worthy of success."

Visualize success: Visualization is an effective strategy for overcoming limiting thoughts. Visualize yourself reaching your goals and the actions you'll need to take to get there. This may assist you in overcoming self-doubt and gaining confidence in your talents.

Take action: Taking action is the key to breaking free from limiting beliefs. Begin taking modest actions toward your goals, even if they are painful or difficult. This might assist you in gaining momentum and confidence in your talents.

Seek help: Breaking through limiting beliefs may be difficult, so seeking help from others is necessary. Discuss your goals and the beliefs holding you back with friends, family, or a coach. They may provide motivation, accountability, and perspective.

Self-compassion: Overcoming limiting beliefs may be a challenging and emotional process. It's important to exercise self-compassion and kindness to oneself along the path. Remember that improvement takes time and that making errors is normal. Instead of concentrating on your limits, concentrate on your development and growth. Celebrate tiny victories and milestones along the road as an incentive to keep going.

Keep trying: Breaking through limiting beliefs is an ongoing process, not a one-time occurrence. It takes perseverance, patience, and a development attitude. Continue pushing yourself beyond your comfort zone, and remember that every stride forward is a step closer to your goals.

Finally, breaking through limiting beliefs is vital in achieving our goals and reaching our full potential. We may overcome self-doubt and create confidence in our skills by identifying our limiting beliefs, confronting them, and replacing them with empowering ones. We may overcome our limits and achieve with perseverance, patience, and a development mentality. We can overcome our limitations and attain achievement.

THE SCIENTIFIC BASIS OF VISUALIZATION AND POSITIVE THINKING

Positive thinking and visualization are key tools for achieving our goals and overcoming challenges. They can alter our thinking, and our viewpoint influences Our behaviors and consequences. The science underlying positive thinking and visualization is based on neuroscience and psychology concepts.

Neuroplasticity is the brain's capacity to alter and adapt in response to experiences and environmental influences. It's the basis for positive thinking and visualization. When we think about positive outcomes, we generate new neural relationships in our brains. These pathways strengthen good ideas and emotions while weakening negative ones. Positive thinking becomes a habit, and our brain rewires to think more favorably.

The act of forming a mental picture of a desired goal is known as visualization. It is based on the idea that the brain cannot distinguish between a vividly imagined and a genuine event. When we imagine a happy result, our brain stimulates the identical areas as it would in real life. This causes the production of neurotransmitters like dopamine, which provide pleasurable feelings and encourage action.

Positive thinking and visualization have been demonstrated in studies to have major advantages for our mental and physical health. Positive thinking has been related to decreased levels of stress and anxiety, as well as enhanced mood and resilience. Visualization has been found to improve performance in various situations, including athletics, public speaking, and academic tests.

In research by the University of California, Los Angeles, basketball players were separated into three groups. One group practiced free throws, another imagined making free throws, while the third did nothing. The group who pictured themselves making free throws improved their accuracy nearly as much as the group that practiced.

Another research from the University of Oxford found that individuals with chronic pain who envisioned the pain being reduced had a drop in pain intensity when compared to those who did not visualize.

Positive thinking and visualization also greatly influence our interpersonal relationships and interactions. We are more inclined to approach social events with an open mind and a pleasant attitude when we think favorably. This may result in improved communication, stronger relationships, and more social support.

However, it is crucial to remember that positive thinking and visualization are not a miracle cure for all our issues. They are not a replacement for action or effort. Positive thinking and visualization may give the inspiration and mentality required for success, but we must still take action and strive toward our goals. It is also critical to strike a balance between optimistic thinking and actuality. Unrealistic expectations and disillusionment may result from blind optimism. It is critical to anticipate potential hurdles and problems and prepare appropriately.

Positive thinking and visualization are strong tools that may assist us in achieving our goals and overcoming challenges. They are based on neuroscience and psychology concepts and have been demonstrated to offer considerable advantages for our mental and physical health. However, it is important to note that positive thinking and visualization are not a panacea for our issues. They are an attitude and drive that must be accompanied by action and effort. We may utilize positive thinking and visualization to unleash our real potential if we have a growth mindset and a dedication to personal progress.

METHODS FOR DEVELOPING A POSITIVE ATTITUDE

A positive attitude is a state of mind centered on optimism, hope, and positivity. It recognizes the positive in every circumstance, even when faced with difficulties and hardship. A positive mentality is vital for self-improvement since it may help you overcome barriers and accomplish your goals. This part will look at several methods for building a positive mentality.

Gratitude Practice

Practicing thankfulness is one of the most effective methods to create a happy mentality. Gratitude is the practice of concentrating on the things in our lives for which we are thankful, and it has been demonstrated to have several advantages, including greater happiness, improved relationships, and improved physical health. Spend a few minutes each day to jot down three things you are thankful for to practice gratitude. This might range from a nice cup of coffee in the morning to a helpful friend or family member.

Positive Self-Talk

Positive self-talk is another method for building a positive mentality. Our ideas profoundly influence our emotions and behavior, and we may alter our attitudes by changing our thinking. Positive self-talk is the practice of replacing negative ideas with positive ones. Instead of thinking, "I can't do this," try thinking, "I am capable and will give it my all." We may build a more optimistic mentality by positively reframing our ideas.

Meditation for Mindfulness

The practice of mindfulness meditation entails concentrating on the present moment without judgment. It has been demonstrated to provide a variety of advantages, including stress reduction, enhanced attention, and improved emotional control. Create a more pleasant and calm mentality by practicing mindfulness meditation daily.

Visualization

Visualization is how you see yourself accomplishing your goals and experiencing pleasant consequences. You may teach your mind to concentrate on the positive rather than the negative by envisioning achievement and positive results. This helps you in developing a more positive and hopeful outlook.

Positive affirmations

Affirmations are phrases you repeat to encourage positive thinking and self-empowerment. They may assist in combating negative self-talk and cultivating a more optimistic outlook. "I am worthy and deserving of love," "I trust in my abilities," and "I choose to focus on the positive" are some examples of positive affirmations.

Surround Yourself with Positive People

The individuals we associate with may have a major influence on our thinking. Surround yourself with pleasant, encouraging, and inspiring people to build a happy outlook. Look for partnerships based on mutual respect, encouragement, and progress.

Negative Beliefs Must Be Challenged

Negative ideas might prevent us from reaching our greatest potential. It is critical to confront negative beliefs and replace them with good ones to create a positive mentality. For example, if you feel incapable of completing a goal, question that idea by emphasizing your prior triumphs and favorable characteristics.

Self-care is essential

Self-care is critical for developing a good outlook. Make time for things that delight you, such as exercise, hobbies, or outside time. To build a more happy and balanced perspective, attend to your bodily, emotional, and spiritual needs.

Concentrate on Solutions, Not Problems

When confronted with a problem, it's tempting to concentrate on the bad elements and linger on the issue. Instead, concentrate on solutions to build a more optimistic outlook. Look for possibilities for development and learning, and concentrate on how you can overcome the obstacle.

Accept Failure as a Learning Experience

Failure is an unavoidable component of the learning process. Accept failure as a chance to learn and develop to create a more optimistic outlook.

Visualization is a great technique for achieving your goals because it activates your imagination and creates a clear mental picture of your goals. When you visualize your goals, you are sending a signal to your subconscious mind, which may then assist you in attracting the resources and chances needed to make your aspirations a reality. In this part, we'll look at various visualization exercises that might help you reach your goals.

Create a Vision Board.

A vision board is a tool for creating a visual representation of your aims and ambitions. You may make a vision board using a bulletin board or a poster and cut out images and statements that symbolize your ambitions. You might add images of locations you wish to visit, individuals you like, or goals you want to accomplish. Display your vision board in a visible location, such as your bedroom or workplace, and spend a few minutes each day imagining yourself attaining your goals.

Mental Rehearsal

Mental rehearsal is a visualization method that includes mentally seeing oneself executing a task or reaching a goal. Mental rehearsal may help you prepare for a certain event, such as a job interview or a performance, or it can help you construct a mental picture of yourself attaining a specific objective. Find a quiet area to relax and shut your eyes to employ mental rehearsal. Use all of your senses to create a vivid mental picture of yourself completing the work or accomplishing the objective. Consider yourself successful, confident, and powerful.

Guided Imagery

Guided imagery is a visualization in which you follow a script or audio that leads you through a particular visualization practice. Guided imagery may help you reach various goals, including stress reduction, improved sleep, and increased confidence. You may obtain guided imagery recordings online or use a recording device or app.

Future Self Visualization

Imagine yourself as the person you want to be as you practice future self-visualization. Find a peaceful spot to relax and shut your eyes to perform this method. Consider yourself in the future, living the life you want and accomplishing your goals. Using all of your senses, create a vivid mental picture of yourself feeling joyful, content, and powerful.

Positive Self-Talk

Positive self-talk is a great strategy for overcoming self-doubt and negative thought habits. Choose a positive affirmation or mantra that resonates with you to utilize positive self-talk, such as "I am capable and worthy of success." Throughout the day, repeat the affirmation to yourself multiple times, imagining yourself attaining your goals and feeling confident and powerful.

Mental Contrasting

Mental contrasting is a visualization method that entails seeing your perfect future and then visualizing the potential hurdles and problems that may happen along the route. Find a quiet spot to relax and shut your eyes to practice mental contrasting. Envision yourself attaining your goals, then envision the hurdles and problems that may emerge. Imagine yourself conquering these challenges and feeling even more powerful and driven to attain your goals.

Emotions Visualization

Emotion visualization is imagining yourself feeling the emotions associated with reaching your goals. Find a peaceful spot to relax and shut your eyes to perform this method. Visualize yourself attaining your goals and feeling the feelings that come with achievement, such as pleasure, pride, and fulfillment. Allow yourself to fully feel the happy emotions involved with attaining your goals by using all of your senses to build a vivid mental picture.

Finally, visualization exercises help you reach your goals by stimulating your imagination and establishing a clear mental picture of what you want to achieve.

Affirmations are a powerful tool for shifting your perspective and overcoming limiting beliefs. They are positive affirmations that you may repeat to yourself to reinforce good thoughts and build a better self-image. Affirmations change your brain by rewiring it and replacing negative thinking patterns with good ones.

Here are some measures to take while utilizing affirmations to change your mind:

Recognize limiting Beliefs: The first step in properly employing affirmations is recognizing the limiting beliefs holding you back. These ideas might be conscious or subconscious, resulting from prior events, negative self-talk, or cultural training. You may develop affirmations to challenge these ideas after you've identified them.

Make positive affirmations: Once you've recognized your limiting thoughts, make positive affirmations to counteract them. These affirmations should be in the current tense, contain positive language, and be situation-specific. For example, if you have a limiting belief that you are not good enough to achieve, you may construct an affirmation that says, "I am worthy of success and capable of achieving my goals."

Repeat affirmations regularly: To get the advantages of affirmations, they must be repeated regularly. You may repeat them quietly to yourself, speak them out, or write them down. Some individuals find it beneficial to develop a daily affirmation practice in which they repeat affirmations at specified times, such as first thing in the morning or before bed.

Visualize your affirmations: Visualizing your affirmations will help reinforce their positive message. When repeating your affirmations, see yourself already having accomplished your goals or being the person you want to be. This might help you construct a more vivid mental image of your desired goal and strengthen your affirmations.

Affirmations must be used in connection with action: Affirmations alone will not result in change. It is critical to behave toward your goals while repeating your affirmations. This might assist you in gaining momentum and reinforcing the good message of your affirmations.

Believe in your affirmations: Finally, to get the advantages of affirmations, you must believe in them. If you repeat affirmations but do not fully believe in them, they will have little effect. Believe in the power of affirmations and their ability to help you transform your perspective and overcome limiting beliefs.

Finally, affirmations are a great tool for shifting your perspective and overcoming limiting beliefs. You may develop positive affirmations that challenge your limiting beliefs, repeat them often, picture them, take action toward your goals, and trust in their power by following the above mentioned steps. Affirmations, with practice, may help you develop a more positive self-image, boost your confidence, and accomplish your goals.

Positive thinking may help you improve your mental health, increase your happiness, and achieve your goals. However, maintaining a cheerful attitude is not always simple, particularly when facing obstacles and losses. Here are some simple ways to incorporate positive thinking into your everyday routine:

Begin the day with a cheerful attitude: Because your morning routine sets the tone for the rest of the day, it's critical to begin with a good attitude. Take a few moments before leaving bed to reflect on your blessings and establish good wishes for the day ahead. You may also read inspirational quotations or affirmations to start your day on the right foot.

Practice gratitude: Gratitude is a strong skill for enhancing happiness and optimism. Spend some time each day reflecting on what you're thankful for and writing it down in a diary. This might help you change your emphasis away from what you don't have and onto what you do have, allowing you to enjoy the little things in life.

Surround yourself with positive people: The individuals you associate with may significantly influence your outlook. Surround yourself with people who are positive, supportive, and who elevate and encourage you. Reduce your exposure to bad news and media by seeking good and inspirational information.

Challenge negative thoughts: Negative thoughts may significantly impede constructive thinking. When you recognize a bad idea, question it by asking yourself whether it's true. Look for facts to back up a more optimistic view and recast negative ideas into positive ones. Affirmations are positive phrases you repeat to reinforce good thoughts and attitudes. Choose affirmations that speak to you and repeat them throughout the day, particularly when feeling sad or stressed.

Concentrate on solutions, not problems: When confronted with a problem or issue, it's easy to get mired in pessimism and despair. Instead, concentrate on finding answers and taking action. Divide the issue into smaller, more achievable stages, and concentrate on what you can do to move ahead.

Celebrate minor victories: minor victories help you gain momentum and keep a good outlook. Take time to celebrate and appreciate your accomplishments when you achieve a little objective or progress toward a bigger one.

Self-care: Taking care of your physical and mental health is critical for having a good mentality. Schedule time for exercise, meditation, and other self-care activities that will help you refresh and remain focused.

Give back to others: Giving back to others may be a great strategy to boost optimism and happiness. Volunteer your time or make a charitable donation to make a difference in the lives of others.

Learn from challenges: Challenges and setbacks are unavoidable, but they may also serve as chances for development and learning. Rather than concentrating on the bad, consider what you can learn from the event and how you can use it to develop and become better.

Positive thinking takes time and work to incorporate into your daily routine, but the advantages are well worth it. You may remain happy even during problems and disappointments by practicing thankfulness, questioning negative ideas, and concentrating on solutions. Remember to appreciate your accomplishments and to look for yourself along the road.

How to set SMART goals

Setting goals is an important part of self-improvement. Goals provide us with focus, direction, and a feeling of purpose. However, not all goals are created equal. Some are hazy and unrealistic, but others are precise, measurable, attainable, relevant, time-bound, or SMART goals.

The abbreviation SMART is specified, measurable, attainable, relevant, and time-bound. Let's take a deeper look at each SMART goal component.

Specific: A purpose that is clear and straightforward. It answers the following questions: who, what, when, where, and why. A specified aim should be well-defined and simple to grasp. Instead of expressing, "I want to be healthier," a more precise aim may be, "I want to lose 10 pounds by the end of the month by exercising four times a week and avoiding processed foods."

Measurable: A measurable aim may be quantified. It helps you track your progress and see whether you're making headway toward your goal. It provides a solution: "How will I know when I've met my goal?" Instead of stating, "I want to improve my public speaking," a quantifiable objective might be, "By the end of the month, I want to give a five-minute speech without notes in front of a group of 20 people."

Achievable: An aim that is reasonable and attainable. It takes into account your present talents and resources and sets a demanding but not unattainable objective. An attainable goal might be "I want to run a 5K in three months by running three times a week and gradually increasing my distance," rather than "I want to run a marathon next week."

Relevant: Relevant goals are significant and match your beliefs, interests, and long-term goals. It answers the question, "Why is this goal important to me?" A more relevant objective might be, "I want to learn how to play the guitar so that I can perform at my friend's wedding in six months."

Time: A time-bound aim has a deadline. It instills a feeling of urgency and keeps you motivated and focused. A time-bound aim might be "I want to write a 50,000-word novel in three months by writing 1,667 words per day" rather than "I want to write a book someday."

Now that we've covered the components, let's look at how to establish a SMART objective.

Step 1: Determine your aim. What do you hope to accomplish? Be detailed and concise.

Step 2: Make a list of your goals. Writing out your objective makes it more real and concrete.

Step 3: Ensure that your aim is SMART. Use the SMART criteria to ensure your objective is precise, measurable, attainable, relevant, and time-bound.

Step 4: Divide your objective into smaller, more doable tasks. What precise activities must you take to reach your goal?

Step 5: Make a plan of action. What precise measures must you take to reach your goal? When are you going to take each step? Who will be there for you along the way?

Step 6: Establish a deadline. When do you wish to accomplish your goal?

Step 7: Keep track of your progress. Check in on your progress regularly and change your strategy as required.

To summarize, creating SMART goals is an effective strategy to attain your personal and professional goals. You may boost your odds of success and remain motivated by being clear, quantifiable, doable, relevant, and time-bound. Remember to divide your goals into small segments, develop an action plan, and measure your progress. You can do everything you put your mind to with persistence and attention.

THE IMPORTANCE OF DIVIDING LARGE GOALS INTO SMALLER ONES

It is easy to feel enthusiastic and ambitious while setting goals and shooting for the stars with high and ambitious dreams. However, it is critical to Recognize that reaching large goals is a lengthy and difficult process that demands persistent work and dedication. Breaking down large goals into smaller ones may help us keep focused, motivated, and on track, increasing our chances of achievement. Breaking down large goals into smaller ones may benefit us in various ways.

For starters, it makes our goals more reasonable and attainable. When we divide a large objective into smaller, bite-sized bits, we may see a clear route to accomplishment and are more inclined to act on our goals. If we want to write a book, breaking it down into smaller goals, like writing a particular number of pages per day or finishing a chapter per week, makes the process more manageable and less intimidating.

Second, breaking down large goals into smaller ones helps us track our progress and stay motivated. It might be difficult to notice progress when we have a long-term objective, particularly in the early stages. When we divide it into smaller goals, we can measure our progress and celebrate minor victories, which may improve our motivation and keep us going. For example, if we want to run a marathon, having smaller goals like jogging 30 minutes daily or finishing a 10k event might help us remain motivated and measure our progress.

Third, breaking down large goals into smaller ones lets us detect possible roadblocks and hurdles early on. We can predict probable obstacles and establish tactics to overcome them when we have a clear strategy. Setting smaller goals, such as lowering sugar consumption or increasing exercise, might help us recognize possible hurdles, such as a hectic work schedule or social obligations, and build tactics to overcome them.

However, breaking down large goals into smaller ones might bring some difficulties. It may be difficult to break down a large objective into smaller ones, and we may feel discouraged or frustrated if we do not see fast progress. These obstacles, however, may be addressed by using effective goal-setting tools, such as the SMART goal framework, and by remaining focused and motivated.

The SMART goal framework, which stands for Specific, Measurable, Achievable, Relevant, and Time-bound, may be used to break down a large objective into smaller ones.

Specific goals are clear and exact; Measurable goals are measurable; Achievable goals are attainable; Relevant goals are associated with our values and priorities; and Time-bound goals have a specific deadline.

Using the SMART goal framework, we can build a clear plan and strategy for accomplishing our goals. For example, if we want to save $10,000 for a down payment on a home, we may divide it into smaller, SMART goals like saving $1,000 each month for ten months or cutting monthly costs by $500 to save $5,000 in six months. Smaller goals that are detailed, quantifiable, realistic, relevant, and time-bound might assist us in tracking our progress and staying motivated.

Finally, breaking down large goals into smaller ones is a great technique for success. It helps us monitor our progress and remain motivated by making our goals more accessible and feasible, and it allows us to recognize possible roadblocks and problems early on. We can overcome any hurdles and accomplish our goals by using good goal-setting procedures and being focused and motivated.

Remember that reaching huge goals requires time, patience, and dedication, but we may boost our chances of success by breaking them down into smaller ones.

FORMULATING AN ACTION PLAN TO ACHIEVE YOUR GOALS

Setting goals is vital to success, but it is just the beginning. To reach your goals, you must develop a plan describing your actions to get there. This strategy will keep you focused and motivated while providing a clear route to follow as you work toward your goals.

The first step in developing an action plan is to divide your objective into smaller, more doable chunks. This will help you stay calm and simplify tracking your progress. Begin by outlining the exact activities you must do to reach your objective. For example, if you aim to run a marathon, some measures you may need to take include increasing your weekly mileage, strength training, and eating a nutritious diet.

Once you've selected the steps you need to perform, rank them in order of relevance and influence on your ultimate aim. This will allow you to concentrate your time and efforts on the most important stages first. If you're training for a marathon, increasing your mileage once a week would be a greater priority than strength training since it directly affects your ability to run the distance.

After prioritizing your action tasks, you should assign deadlines to each one. This will assist you in staying on track and making progress toward your objective. Set realistic deadlines that are both doable and will motivate you to work towards your objective.

Once you've determined your action steps and deadlines, it's time to devise a strategy for carrying them out. This might entail scheduling exercise time, developing a diet plan, or finding a training partner to hold you responsible.

Consider any potential hurdles or problems and devise a strategy to overcome them. For example, if you are preparing for a marathon in the winter, you may need to modify your training schedule to allow for bad weather.

Keeping track of your progress as you work toward your objective is also critical. This will keep you motivated and give you a feeling of success as you meet each goal. Track your success using a notebook, planner, or app, and change your strategy as required.

Finally, being adaptable and open to changing your strategy as you go is critical. Life is unpredictably unpredictable, and things do not always happen as planned. Be willing to change your strategy while remaining focused on your primary aim.

In conclusion, developing an action plan is critical to achieving your goals. You can stay on track and make consistent progress toward your objective by breaking down your goal into smaller, achievable stages, prioritizing those actions, establishing deadlines, making a plan, measuring your progress, and being adaptable. If you have a well-crafted action plan, you may remain motivated, focused, and confident that you are taking the essential actions to attain your goals.

TIPS FOR STAYING MOTIVATED AND TRACKING PROGRESS

Keeping motivated is essential for reaching your goals and keeping on track with your personal development path.

However, maintaining motivation can be challenging, particularly when faced with hurdles or disappointments along the road. That's why it's critical to have tactics to keep you motivated and monitor your success. Here are some pointers to help you remain motivated and monitor your success on your personal development journey.

Set clear, quantifiable goals: Setting explicit, measurable goals is one of the greatest methods to remain motivated.

It's simpler to remain focused and motivated when you know what you want to accomplish. Make your goals explicit and quantifiable to measure your progress and see how far you've gone.

Divide your ambitions into smaller, more doable tasks:

Our ambitions often seem daunting or out of reach. That is why dividing them into smaller, more doable jobs is critical.

This will help you keep focused and motivated since you can observe improvement in smaller, more manageable increments.

Celebrate your victories: Recognizing and celebrating your victories along the road may be a tremendous motivation. Take the time to recognize and appreciate each accomplishment, no matter how minor. This will keep you motivated and cheerful even when things become difficult.

Find a partner to keep you responsible: Having someone to hold you accountable may be a terrific motivation. Find a friend, family member, or coach who can help you remain on track and give encouragement and support along the journey.

Use visualization methods: Visualization techniques may be a great motivator. Spend some time visualizing yourself attaining your goals and feeling successful. This helps you to be motivated and focused on your goals.

Maintain a diary: Keeping a journal may help you measure your development and reflect on your growth journey. List your goals, achievements, obstacles, and any insights you discover. This might assist you in being motivated and focused on your goals.

Surround yourself with good people: Surrounding yourself with positive people can help you remain motivated and focused on your goals. Seek out friends, family members, or coworkers who will encourage and support you on your personal development path.

Use positive affirmations: Positive affirmations may be a very effective motivator. Spend some time each day repeating to yourself positive affirmations such as "I am capable of achieving my goals" or "I am deserving of success." This might help you remain motivated and cheerful even when faced with difficulties.

Seek inspiration from those who have accomplished similar goals: Seeking inspiration from others who have achieved similar goals may be a terrific motivator. Read books, listen to podcasts, or attend events pertinent to your personal development path. This might help you keep motivated while learning from others who have had similar situations.

Track progress with technology: Technology may be a wonderful tool for monitoring progress and remaining motivated. Track your progress toward your goals using applications or online tools, set reminders, or connect with others on a similar personal development path.

By applying these ideas, you can remain motivated and measure your success on your personal development journey. Remember that remaining motivated is an ongoing process, and it's normal to have ups and downs along the road. Celebrate your victories, learn from your setbacks, and never give up on your dreams.

Overcoming Setbacks and Modifying Your Strategy as Necessary

Obstacles are unavoidable when attaining our goals and chasing our aspirations. They may be depressing and unpleasant, and they might make us want to give up. On the other hand, obstacles are a natural part of the trip, and they present possibilities for development and learning. In this part, we'll talk about overcoming challenges and changing your strategy to keep on track.

The first step in overcoming barriers is to recognize and accept them. This may seem contradictory, given that our natural tendency is to fight and avoid barriers. Denying or disregarding challenges, on the other hand, might lead to emotions of worry, anxiety, and overload. We may change our emphasis from what isn't working to finding answers and moving ahead by identifying and embracing challenges.

The next stage is to shift your perspective. Instead of seeing hurdles as impediments to your achievement, consider their chances for development and learning. Every challenge you face is an opportunity to strengthen your resilience, learn new skills, and acquire important experience. Changing your mindset may convert hurdles into stepping stones to your ambitions.

After you've reframed your mentality, it's time to devise a strategy. This entails recognizing the particular problem and brainstorming possible remedies. Be bold and think creatively and beyond the box. Sometimes, the finest answers are the ones that seem unusual or hazardous.

It is also important to seek help from others. This may take numerous forms, including contacting a mentor, networking with like-minded people, or employing a coach or consultant. As you navigate hurdles, having a support system may give you vital insights, comments, and encouragement.

It is critical to be flexible and change your strategy while attempting to overcome hurdles. This entails being willing to pivot, adjust your emphasis, or attempt a different strategy. Remember that the road to success is seldom a straight one. It is natural to have setbacks and difficulties along the route. You may overcome hurdles and stay on track to your goals by being flexible and adaptive.

In certain circumstances, overcoming a hurdle may require a considerable strategy adjustment or even a total shift in direction. This might be challenging, particularly if you've put a lot of time and effort into a certain approach. However, remember that your ultimate aim is not the journey but the destination. If the road you're on isn't working, it's alright to change course and try something different. It may be required to attain your goals.

In conclusion, overcoming difficulties is an inevitable aspect of the self-improvement path. You may overcome hurdles and stay on track to your goals by admitting and embracing them, reframing your mentality, making a plan of action, seeking help, being flexible, and revising your plan as required. Remember that the path to success is seldom straight. It is natural to have setbacks and difficulties along the route. However, with determination and a development attitude, you can overcome any barrier and accomplish your goals.

CHAPTER 4: PRODUCTIVITY AND TIME MANAGEMENT TECHNIQUES

THE SIGNIFICANCE OF SETTING TIME PRIORITIES

Time is a valuable and limited resource, and how we prioritize and use it has a big influence on our personal and professional life. Many of us have hectic lives, combining job, family, social obligations, and personal interests. It's natural to feel stressed and as if there aren't enough hours in the day to get everything done. That is why it is critical to efficiently prioritize your time.

Prioritizing your time entails making deliberate decisions about how you spend your time. It entails determining your top priorities and spending your time and energy appropriately. When we prioritize our time, we can concentrate on what is essential and make progress toward our goals rather than being mired down in irrelevant or inconsequential duties.

Identifying your goals and values is one of the most important stages in allocating your time. What do you hope to accomplish? What matters most to you in your personal and professional life? By answering these questions, you may obtain clarity and concentrate on what is most important to you.

After you've determined your goals and values, you may allocate your time appropriately. This entails deciding how to spend your time depending on what is most important to you. For example, if spending time with your family is a major priority, you can reduce your work hours or delegate certain tasks to make more time for them. It is also important to be realistic about how much time you have available and how long it will take to complete particular tasks.

Many of us have a propensity to overcommit or underestimate the amount of time required to finish a job. This may result in tension, exhaustion, and a sense of being always behind. You may establish more feasible goals and feel more in control of your schedule if you are realistic about the time you have available and the time it takes to finish a job.

Another important part of time management is learning to say no. It may be difficult to decline pleas or opportunities, particularly when they come from individuals we care about or respect. Saying yes to everything, on the other hand, may lead to overcommitment and a lack of concentration on our goals. Learning to say no may be liberating because it allows us to concentrate on what is actually important and avoid spending time on things that do not line with our goals and beliefs.

In addition to saying no, it is critical to prevent distractions and multitasking. Distractions abound in today's environment, from social media updates to email alerts and text messages. As we strive to fit as many tasks into a day as possible, multitasking might be attractive. Distractions and multitasking, on the other hand, may lead to a loss of attention and lower productivity. You may boost your productivity and do more in less time by removing distractions and concentrating on one activity at a time.

Finally, it is important to prioritize self-care and take care of yourself. Many of us prioritize work or other duties above our personal needs. Neglecting our physical and mental health, on the other hand, may lead to burnout and a reduced capacity to concentrate and be productive. You may enhance your general well-being and your capacity to prioritize your time by creating time for exercise, relaxation, and other self-care activities.

Finally, prioritizing your time is critical for personal and professional success. You may concentrate on the things that matter most and accomplish your goals by recognizing your goals and values, being realistic about your time, learning to say no, removing distractions and avoiding multitasking, and prioritizing self-care. Remember that time is a limited resource, therefore make the most of it by carefully prioritizing your time.

METHODS FOR CREATING A DAILY ROUTINE THAT SUITS YOU

Creating a daily plan that works for you might take time and effort. With so many activities and obligations to manage, it may take a lot of work to strike a balance that enables you to be productive while prioritizing your time and well-being. In this part, we'll look at practical ways to create a daily routine that works for you.

Begin with a Brain Dump

It's a good idea to start with a brain dump before making your daily routine. Take a few moments to jot down any tasks, appointments, or duties that occur to mind. Work duties, domestic tasks, personal appointments, and everything else that has to be completed fall under this category. It's much simpler to prioritize and arrange your duties after you've written everything down.

Organize Your Tasks

Once you've identified all of your tasks, it's time to prioritize them. Determine which tasks are the most urgent or vital and prioritize them. These are the items you should prioritize on your to-do list. Consider which tasks are time-sensitive and must be finished on a given day or time and which can wait.

Make use of a Time Block Schedule

A time block plan is a common scheduling strategy in which you divide your day into time blocks and assign particular activities to each block. For example, you may set out two hours in the morning for work-related duties, an hour for exercise, and another for domestic tasks. You may better organize your time and prevent distractions by designating specified blocks of time for each work.

Include Rest Periods

It is essential to pause throughout the day to recharge and prevent burnout. Include brief pauses in your schedule, such as a 10-minute walk or stretching exercise between duties. This will allow you to remain focused and productive while allowing your brain and body to relax and rejuvenate.

Be practical

Being realistic about what you can do while setting your daily agenda is important. Don't overburden yourself with tasks or set unreasonable deadlines. If you cannot finish everything on your list, this will only lead to tension and disappointment. Instead, concentrate on the most critical activities and prioritize them properly.

Learn to Say No

One of the most difficult aspects of having a daily plan is learning to say no. It's critical to realize when you're taking on too much and to learn to avoid new responsibilities or obligations. This will help you prevent burnout and concentrate on the most critical activities.

Take Advantage of Technology

Several productivity tools and applications are available to assist you in staying organized and managing your time successfully. Consider utilizing a calendar software to set appointments and reminders or a task management tool to keep track of your tasks. Utilizing a time monitoring tool could also be useful to keep track of how you spend your time during the day.

Prepare for Unexpected Occurrences

Unexpected incidents are unavoidable, no matter how carefully you organize your day. Leaving some room in your calendar for unanticipated occurrences or crises is critical. This might include allowing additional time between jobs or having a backup plan in case anything unexpected occurs.

Be willing to make changes

Creating a daily routine is a continuous effort, and flexibility is important. Be bold and adjust if your existing routine isn't working for you. Adjust your timetable or experiment with various strategies until you discover what works best.

Examine and Consider

Take some time at the end of each day to review your schedule and reflect on what went well and what may be improved.

STRATEGIES FOR GETTING RID OF DISTRACTIONS AND PROCRASTINATION

Procrastination and distractions are two of the most important roadblocks to accomplishing one's goals. They may be a major cause of irritation and contribute to a loss of productivity, which can impact our mental health and general well-being. Overcoming procrastination and distractions is essential for success in every area of life, whether personal or professional.

In this part, we will look at practical techniques and tactics to help you overcome procrastination and distractions and accomplish your goals.

Identify the root of procrastination: Identifying the underlying cause of procrastination is the first step in conquering it. Fear of failure, a lack of drive, or a lack of defined goals may all contribute to procrastination. Understanding the fundamental reason for your procrastination will allow you to devise solutions to overcome it.

Divide jobs into smaller steps: Individuals delay because they are overwhelmed by the work at hand. Tasks may be made less frightening and simpler to complete by breaking them down into smaller, more manageable pieces. This might assist you in staying motivated and on track.

Set deadlines: Setting deadlines might assist you in being responsible and motivated. You are more likely to prioritize your duties and avoid procrastinating if you have a definite deadline to achieve. Make careful to establish reasonable and attainable timeframes.

Remove distractions: One of the leading causes of procrastination is distraction. Distractions, whether social media, email alerts, or phone calls, may break your attention and hinder you from completing your work. Turn off alerts and use programs that block distracting websites to reduce distractions as much as possible.

Use the Pomodoro Technique: The Pomodoro Technique is a time-management strategy that may assist you in overcoming procrastination and increasing your productivity. It entails dividing your work into 25-minute increments, followed by brief pauses. This strategy may assist you in staying focused and avoiding burnout.

Reward yourself after finishing a task: Rewarding oneself after completing a task may be a great motivator. It might help you keep focused and on track if you know there will be a reward at the end. Ensure the reward is something you love and appropriate to the work you completed.

Practice mindfulness: Mindfulness is a wonderful skill for dealing with distractions and procrastination. By practicing mindfulness, train your mind to concentrate on the current moment and avoid being sidetracked by irrelevant ideas. This helps you to be focused and productive.

Make your atmosphere conducive: Your environment may significantly influence your productivity. Ensure your desk is tidy, well-organized, and without distractions. You may also include items that motivate you, such as inspirational quotations or photographs.

Use positive self-talk: Negative self-talk is a major driver of procrastination. You are more inclined to avoid something if you repeatedly convince yourself you can't do it. Positive self-talk may assist you in remaining motivated and overcoming problems.

Get an accountability partner: Having someone hold you responsible may be a strong incentive. Find an accountability partner who shares your goals and can assist you in staying on track. You may schedule frequent check-ins to review your progress and exchange procrastination-busting methods.

To summarize, overcoming procrastination and distractions is crucial to success in every part of life. You may overcome procrastination and distractions by recognizing the root of your procrastination, reducing activities into smaller pieces, establishing deadlines, avoiding distractions, and using practical strategies such as the Pomodoro Technique and mindfulness. Remember to be patient and persistent; overcoming procrastination and diversions requires commitment and effort.

TASK DELEGATION AND WORKFLOW OPTIMIZATION

Delegating tasks and optimizing processes are two essential skills for anybody trying to increase productivity and accomplish their goals. The ability to delegate successfully frees up your time and allows you to better use the talents and abilities of your team members. Streamlining your workflow, on the other hand, assists you in identifying and eliminating needless activities, reducing lost time, and improving overall efficiency. This part will cover how to efficiently delegate duties and optimize your workflow to obtain better outcomes.

How to Effectively Delegate Tasks

Delegating work is more than simply giving responsibilities to others; it is about enabling your team members to take ownership and contribute to the project's or organization's success. Here are some pointers on how to successfully assign tasks:

Determine which duties to delegate: You must choose which task to delegate before delegating any assignment.

Look for time-consuming jobs that do not meet your core competency or need another team member's expertise.

Choose the best individual for the job: When delegating responsibilities, you must choose the best individual for the job. Before allocating assignments to them, consider their talents, expertise, and availability.

Communicate expectations clearly: When assigning responsibilities, it is critical to convey precisely what you anticipate from the individual. Define the work clearly, specify timelines, and outline the desired results.

Provide all required resources and assistance: Give the individual the necessary resources, tools, and assistance to execute the assignment effectively.

Trust your team members: When assigning duties, you must trust your team members' abilities. Give them agency and the ability to make judgments.

Follow up regularly: Regularly check in with the individual to assess development and give comments.

Success should be celebrated: Celebrate the individual and team's accomplishment. Recognition and gratitude boost morale and motivation.

Organizing Your Workflow

Streamlining your workflow includes:

- Identifying and removing redundant duties.
- Automating procedures.
- Improving your workspace for increased efficiency.

Here are some suggestions for streamlining your workflow:

Determine which tasks bring the greatest value: Identify and prioritize the activities crucial to attaining your goals. Tasks that are unnecessary or bring little value should be eliminated or delegated.

Process automation: Identify jobs that can be automated, such as repetitive tasks, and simplify them using software or technologies.

Improve your working environment: Reduce distractions and organize your work environment to create a workplace that is favorable to productivity.

Make use of technology: Use technology to help you organize your time, such as calendar software for scheduling meetings and deadlines.

Establish deadlines: Set yourself deadlines to help you prioritize tasks and prevent procrastinating.

Take frequent breaks: Breaks may help you refresh and remain focused.

Understand how to say no: Learn to say no to projects that do not correspond to your goals or priorities.

Keep track of your time: Use time-tracking software to track how you spend your time and uncover opportunities for improvement.

Make use of checklists: Make checklists to assist you in staying organized and prioritizing your tasks.

Constantly improve: Evaluate your process regularly and seek methods to enhance it.

Finally, delegating responsibilities and optimizing your workflow is crucial for anybody trying to increase productivity and accomplish their goals. You may get greater outcomes by properly delegating and using the abilities and strengths of your team members. You may improve productivity by simplifying your workflow, eliminating superfluous tasks, automating procedures, and optimizing your work environment.

Technology has transformed the way we work and live our lives. It has also supplied us with many tools and software to help us keep organized and productive. In this part, we'll review some of the most successful methods to employ technology to improve your work processes and increase production.

Time Tracking Apps

One of the most difficult aspects of being productive is managing your time. Time monitoring tools assist you in measuring how you spend your time throughout the day, identifying areas of waste, and optimizing your work plan. Toggl, RescueTime, and Clockify are other popular time monitoring applications.

Task Management Tools

Task management solutions are vital for remaining organized and completing your tasks on schedule. Many applications, such as Asana, Todoist, and Trello, are available to help you build to-do lists, establish deadlines, and assign tasks to team members.

Project Management Software

Project management software is crucial for larger-scale projects with several team members and complicated operations. Basecamp, Monday.com, and Wrike are tools that help you organize projects, interact with team members, and measure progress.

Cloud Storage

Cloud storage is a great way to ensure your information is accessible from any device and backed up in case of data loss. Dropbox, Google Drive, and OneDrive are examples of popular cloud storage companies.

Email Management Tools

Emails may be a major source of distraction and can derail your productivity if they are not handled properly. Tools like Boomerang, SaneBox, and Inbox by Gmail may help you manage your emails, prioritize messages, and create reminders to follow up on critical discussions

Browser Extensions

Browser extensions are extremely useful for increasing productivity and saving time. Grammarly, which analyzes your grammar and spelling in real-time, and Momentum, which offers a gorgeous dashboard with a to-do list and encouraging quotations, may help you remain focused and inspired.

Password Managers

In today's digital age, passwords are an unavoidable evil. However, they might be difficult to manage. LastPass, 1Password, and Dashlane are password managers that may help you establish and save safe passwords and automatically log you into websites.

Online Learning Platforms

Continuous learning is crucial for personal development and job advancement. Online learning sites such as Coursera, Udemy, and LinkedIn Learning provide diverse courses and certifications that may assist you in gaining new skills and information.

Virtual Meetings Tools

As remote work becomes increasingly widespread, virtual conference solutions like Zoom, Microsoft Teams, and Google Meet have become indispensable. These technologies enable you to communicate with team members and customers, collaborate on projects, and hold meetings from anywhere.

Automation Tools

Automation technologies may help you automate monotonous operations, freeing time for more important duties. Automation technologies such as Zapier, IFTTT, and Integromat may help you automate processes and connect various applications and resources.

Finally, technology can change how we work and live. By harnessing the tools and technologies, we can remain organized, increase productivity, and do more in less time. However, it is important to remember that technology is only a tool, and it is up to us to use it best. We may make our lives more efficient and fun by utilizing technology wisely.

Chapter 5: Creating Good Habits and Kicking Bad Ones

Knowledge Of The Science Behind Habit Development

Habits have a strong influence on our lives. They are the subtle, often unconscious behaviors that we do daily, and they may greatly influence our overall success and pleasure. Habits may help us accomplish our goals or hinder us from attaining our greatest potential. Understanding the science of habit development is critical for everyone who wishes to build beneficial and break bad habits.

The idea of neuroplasticity is fundamental to habit development. The capacity of the brain to alter and adapt in response to new experiences is referred to as neuroplasticity. When we repeat an action, our brain establishes neural relationships that make repeating that activity simpler in the future. This is why it is so difficult to change habits; our brain has practically rewired itself to make the action routine. A signal or trigger initiates the habit-building process. This might range from a certain time of day to a specific place or even an emotion. The cue causes the brain to enter a habit loop with three components: the cue, the action, and the reward. The habit is the activity, and the reward is the pleasurable sensation we experience from executing the behavior.

To form a new habit, you must first discover the signal that initiates the desired action. For example, if you want to start exercising every morning, you may lay out your gym clothing the night before as a reminder. The next step is to define the behavior you wish to create. It would be exercising for a certain period every morning in this situation. Finally, you must provide a reward for successfully performing the behavior. This might be a sense of success, a rise in energy, or a simple indulgence like a cup of coffee.

Once you've built your habit loop, you must regularly repeat it over time. According to research, acquiring a new habit takes an average of 66 days. During this period, it is critical to remain dedicated and prevent interrupting the habit loop. When it comes to developing new habits, consistency is essential. Breaking a bad habit follows the same cycle but in the opposite direction. You must determine the cue that causes the action, behavior, and reward. Once you've discovered these aspects, you may break the habit cycle. This might include altering your surroundings or discovering a new habit that gives a comparable reward. For example, If you tend to munch when you're bored, you may try going for a stroll or completing a little exercise instead.

Recognizing the emotional and psychological aspects that might influence habit development is also critical. Negative emotions such as tension, worry, and despair make it more difficult to create new habits, but pleasant emotions such as happiness and joy simplify it. Furthermore, our beliefs and mentality might greatly impact our capacity to create new behaviors. If you feel you can't change, you'll be less inclined to do the work necessary to create new behaviors.

Finally, knowing the science of habit development is critical for anybody who wishes to build beneficial habits and break bad ones. You may build new habits that support your goals and break old ones that hold you back by understanding the trigger, activity, and reward that comprise your habit loop. Remember that habit-building takes time and work, but you can accomplish long-term change with patience and dedication.

TECHNIQUES FOR BUILDING POSITIVE HABITS AND MAKING THEM STICK

Positive buildup of habits is a crucial component of human growth and development. Habits are strong behavioral forces that may make or break our success. However, the issue is more in developing habits than in making them stay. Most of us have been frustrated when we begin a new habit only to discontinue it after a few days or weeks. This part will look at several methods for developing and sustaining beneficial behaviors.

Begin Small

Starting too large is one of individuals' most frequent errors when forming a new habit. They establish grandiose goals and attempt to make big behavioral changes simultaneously.

Unfortunately, this strategy is seldom successful. Instead, begin slowly. Choose one minor habit to work on and concentrate on it. For example, if you wish to start exercising frequently, start with only 10 minutes daily. Once you've mastered that, slowly increase the time.

Be Specific

Make your habit quantifiable and explicit. Instead of a general aim like "I want to exercise more," pick a particular goal like "I want to walk for 30 minutes daily." Being precise makes it easy to track progress and maintain motivation.

Connect a Trigger to Your Habit

Connecting a new habit to an existing trigger is an efficient approach to creating it. If you want to start flossing your teeth daily, link it to an established habit like cleaning your teeth. Floss after brushing your teeth every time. Brushing your teeth will become a trigger for flossing over time, making it simpler to recall.

Use Positive Reinforcement.

Positive reinforcement is a very effective motivator. Reward yourself whenever you fulfill your habit effectively. It might be as basic as a slap on the back or a favorite snack. Celebrating your accomplishments will keep you motivated and perpetuate the habit.

Create a Habit Tracker

A habit tracker is a visual tool that lets you track your progress. It might be a calendar, a graph, or an application. Mark the tracker every time you fulfill your habit successfully. Seeing your success keeps you encouraged and reinforces the habit.

Find an Accountability Partner

Having someone hold you responsible may be an effective motivator. Find someone who shares your aim and keep in touch with them regularly. Share your progress, share problems, and encourage one another to develop good habits.

Practice Mindfulness

Mindfulness is the discipline of being completely involved in what you are doing and being present in the moment. It may assist you in remaining focused and overcoming distractions that disrupt your habit-building attempts. If you spend a few minutes each day practicing mindfulness, you will find it simpler to keep to your routines.

Plan for Obstacles

Obstacles are a regular component of the habit-building process. Anticipate and prepare for probable roadblocks. If you want to exercise daily, plan what you will do if it rains. Having a strategy in place can help you overcome challenges and stick to your habits.

Accept Failure

Forming new habits is not always simple, and setbacks are unavoidable. Failure should not discourage you. Instead, see it as a chance to learn and develop. Examine what went wrong and revise your strategy. Remember that success is about rebounding back from failure, not never failing.

Concentrate on Progress, Not Perfection

Finally, remember that developing beneficial habits is a journey, not a destination. Concentrate on progress rather than perfection. Celebrate modest victories and learn from failures. Be patient and persistent; your beneficial habits will ultimately become a normal part of your everyday routine.

OVERCOMING TYPICAL BARRIERS TO THE DEVELOPMENT OF HABITS.

Developing good habits is an essential aspect of personal development and self-improvement. However, sticking to a new habit might be difficult, particularly if you face regular hurdles. In this part, we will look at some of the most frequent barriers to habit development and provide practical solutions to help you overcome them.

Inadequate motivation

A lack of motivation is one of the most prevalent barriers to habit development. It might be tough to find the desire to begin a new habit, particularly if you don't love it or notice instant advantages from it. To conquer this challenge, you must first determine your why. Ask yourself why you want to start this habit and what advantages it will provide you. This will assist you in remaining motivated and devoted to your new habit.

Another excellent method for increasing motivation is to divide your habit into smaller, more doable tasks. Rather than attempting to tackle a large objective simultaneously, divide it into smaller tasks you may do daily. This will give you a feeling of accomplishment and development, which may be quite motivating.

Lack of Time

A lack of time is another significant impediment to habit development. Many of us have busy lives, and finding the time to form a new habit may be difficult. To solve this challenge, you must focus your time. Make your new habit a priority by incorporating it into your everyday routine. This might include getting up early, limiting other activities, or outsourcing certain work to others.

Eliminating distractions is another excellent technique to get more time. Every day, many of us squander time on things that do not get us closer to our goals. You can make the most of your time and reach your goals faster if you eliminate these distractions and concentrate on your new habit.

Lack of accountability

Accountability is an essential component of habit-building. When held responsible for someone else, we are more likely to adhere to a new behavior. However, many of us struggle with responsibility because we lack accountability or fear failure. It is critical to locate an accountability partner to help you conquer this challenge. This might be a friend, family member, or coach who can assist you in staying on track and providing support when needed.

Tracking your progress is another great technique to increase responsibility. This might be as basic as noting each day on a calendar or utilizing an app to keep track of your progress. Tracking your progress allows you to see how far you've gone and remain inspired to keep going.

Lack of consistency

When it comes to habit building, consistency is everything. If you are inconsistent, making your new habit a permanent part of your routine will be tough. To overcome this barrier, creating and keeping to a routine is critical. Make your new habit an unavoidable part of your daily routine, and do it simultaneously every day. This will assist you in developing a regular habit that will be simpler to maintain in the long term.

Starting small is another excellent method to improve consistency. Rather than attempting to acquire a large habit, begin with a little habit and work your way up. This will assist you in developing a regular habit that will be simpler to maintain over time.

Lack of determination

Willpower is a crucial component in habit building. It requires determination to form and maintain a new habit, particularly when faced with difficulties or temptations. It is critical to practice self-care to overcome this barrier. Ensure you sleep well, eat nutritious food, and look after your mental health.

GIVING UP BAD HABITS AND FORMING GOOD ONES IN THEIR STEAD

Habits are activities that we participate in without thinking about it. They are often developed due to repeated behaviors and may greatly influence our lives. Negative behaviors may harm our health, relationships, and general well-being. Breaking bad habits and replacing them with good ones may be a difficult but necessary component of personal development.

The first step in changing a bad habit is to recognize it. Overeating, smoking, procrastination, and negative self-talk are examples of bad habits. Once you've recognized your bad behavior, you need to understand why you do it. Is it a stress or anxiety coping technique, or is it the consequence of boredom or a lack of direction? Understanding the underlying cause of the habit might assist you in addressing the fundamental problem and developing a strategy for change.

Breaking a bad habit involves dedication and discipline. Setting realistic goals and developing a transition strategy are critical. One useful method is to replace a bad habit with a good one. For example, if you have a bad habit of snacking on unhealthy foods, you might replace it with a healthy option like eating fruits or vegetables. You are still meeting your want for a snack but more pleasantly and helpfully.

Creating a supportive atmosphere is another helpful method. This may include surrounding oneself with good influences and avoiding events or triggers that lead to bad behavior. It may also include requesting help from friends, family, or a professional. Breaking a habit may be difficult, but having a support system might simplify it. It is essential to be patient and persistent and replace bad behaviors with good ones.

Breaking a habit does not happen quickly, and setbacks are typical. It is important to accept and learn from these failures to move ahead. Small triumphs and development also assist in keeping motivation and momentum going.

Developing constructive habits is an important element of human development. Positive habits can enhance our health, relationships, and general well-being. The first step in developing beneficial habits is determining the behaviors you wish to foster. This might be anything from daily exercise to practicing appreciation or learning a new skill.

Once you've defined your desired good habit, you must devise a strategy for implementing it.

Setting precise, measurable goals and developing a daily routine may assist in making the habit a permanent part of your life. Starting small and progressively increasing the difficulty or frequency of the habit may also aid in forming a long-lasting habit.

Developing beneficial habits needs discipline and perseverance. It's critical to stick with the habit, even if it doesn't seem to have much effect. Monitoring progress and celebrating tiny triumphs might be beneficial to sustain motivation and momentum.

In addition to developing good behaviors, it is critical to create a growth mentality. This entails seeing obstacles and failures as chances for development and learning. Adopting a growth mindset may assist you in overcoming hurdles and maintaining a positive attitude toward personal development.

To summarize, changing bad habits and developing good ones is an important element of personal development. It takes dedication, patience, and a willingness to adapt. You may break bad habits and replace them with good ones by recognizing harmful behaviors, understanding the underlying causes, and developing a strategy for change. Positive habit formation entails defining desirable behaviors, developing a strategy for execution, and maintaining consistency and discipline. You may establish good habits and accomplish personal progress by adopting a growth mindset and surrounding yourself with positive influences.

Creating good habits is a powerful approach to enhancing your life, accomplishing your goals, and tapping into your inner strength. However, developing a habit is the first step; sustaining it over time is also vital. In this part, we will look at ways to keep your good habits going in the long run so you may enjoy the advantages of your efforts.

Set realistic goals for yourself.

One of the reasons individuals struggle to keep beneficial behaviors is because they have unreasonable expectations. If you set the bar too high, you may feel disheartened if you don't see immediate results. It's crucial to remember that developing a habit is a gradual process that may take some time to see results. Set reasonable goals for yourself, and don't be disheartened if you don't get instant results.

Celebrate Your Success

It's important to recognize your accomplishments along the road. Take some time to reflect on the good improvements that have resulted from your new behaviors. Celebrating your accomplishments helps keep you motivated and encouraged to continue your path.

Focus on the Benefits

Remember why you began developing beneficial habits in the first place. Concentrate on the advantages you're getting from your new behaviors. This might help you remain motivated and dedicated to keeping your behaviors long-term.

Have a Support System

Having a support system may make a significant difference in your ability to sustain beneficial behaviors over time. Surround yourself with individuals who will encourage and support you on your path. Join a community of like-minded people who are striving to better their lives. Having a support system helps you remain motivated and responsible.

Keep track of your progress

Keeping track of your progress might assist you in remaining motivated and dedicated to keeping your beneficial habits in the long run. Use a habit tracker to measure your progress and celebrate your accomplishments.

Create a Routine

Developing a routine helps you maintain your beneficial behaviors over time. When you stick to a schedule, your habits become established in your everyday life, making it simpler to keep them up over time. Set times for your habits and try to keep to them as much as possible.

Make Adjustments as Needed

Remember that developing a habit is not a one-size-fits-all endeavor. Everyone is unique; what works for one individual may not work for the next. If you discover that your existing technique isn't working, be willing to make changes. Experiment with many tactics until you discover the one that works best for you.

Maintain a Positive Attitude

Maintaining a happy mentality significantly impacts your ability to sustain beneficial behaviors over time. Concentrate on your progress and the rewards you're reaping as a consequence of your new behaviors. Negative self-talk should be avoided and replaced with positive affirmations.

Be ready for setbacks.

Setbacks are an unavoidable part of every journey, including the one to develop beneficial habits. Planning for setbacks and having a strategy to deal with them is critical. Don't be disheartened if you have difficulties. Instead, see them as a chance to learn and develop.

Continue to Learn and Grow

Finally, it is critical to continue learning and improving to sustain your beneficial behaviors over time. Maintain an open mind and a willingness to explore new things. Accept the voyage of personal development and realize it is a lifetime process.

Effective communication is a critical component of personal development and success. Understanding the various communication styles and when to employ them to communicate successfully is essential.

People's communication styles pertain to expressing themselves and connecting with others. Understanding diverse communication styles may help you interact with people more effectively, develop deeper relationships, and accomplish your goals.

Communication styles are classified into four types: passive, aggressive, passive-aggressive, and forceful. Each style has its traits that make it suitable for various contexts.

Passive Communication Style

A lack of assertiveness and a reluctance to communicate one's thoughts or ideas describe a passive communication style. Individuals who utilize this communication style seek to avoid confrontation and give in to others' requests, even if they disagree. Passive communicators may feel helpless or insecure about their capacity to communicate successfully.

This communication approach may be useful when relationship maintenance is more vital than reaching a particular goal. For example, if you're dealing with a problematic client or customer, you can utilize a passive communication approach to avoid escalating the issue.

However, passive communication may be harmful when conveying your demands or thoughts. Others may take advantage of you if you are constantly passive in your communication, or you may feel dissatisfied in your relationships or profession.

Aggressive Communication Style

An aggressive communication style characterizes an emphasis on winning and accomplishing one's own goals at the cost of others. Aggressive communicators may use threats, intimidation, or insults to achieve their goals. This communication style may harm relationships and create a hostile atmosphere.

Aggressive speech may be suitable when you need to assert yourself or protect yourself against a perceived danger. If you are being harassed or bullied, for example, you may need to use forceful speech to defend yourself. Conversely, Aggressive communication may be unproductive and have harmful results. You risk alienating people and damaging your relationships if you consistently employ harsh speech.

Passive-Aggressive Communication Style

A mix of passive and aggressive activities distinguishes a passive-aggressive communication style. Passive-aggressive communicators may conceal their anger or irritation via sarcasm, gossip, or backstabbing. This communication style may be perplexing and can lead to conflict in relationships.

Passive-aggressive speech may be suitable when you wish to convey your displeasure or irritation without immediately approaching the other person. However, this communication style may harm relationships and cause long-term harm.

Assertive Communication Style

The assertive communication style emphasizes expressing one's views and ideas courteously and forthrightly. Assertive communicators may successfully express themselves without being aggressive or submissive. In most cases, this communication approach is the most effective and acceptable.

Assertive communication may be suitable when you need to voice your wants or thoughts, establish limits, or negotiate with others. Mutual respect underpins assertive communication, which may lead to stronger relationships and greater results.

To communicate assertively, use "I" words, convey your emotions clearly, and actively listen to others. Being assertive also entails believing in yourself and your ability to express yourself effectively.

Recognizing the various communication styles and when to apply them is a critical component of personal development and success. You may communicate more effectively, develop better relationships, and accomplish your goals by knowing your communication style and the styles of others.

Empathy and strong listening abilities are crucial components of successful communication. When we actively listen and demonstrate empathy, we create an atmosphere where people feel heard, appreciated, and understood. In this part, we will look at the value of excellent listening abilities and how to demonstrate empathy in our relationships with others.

Effective listening is more than just hearing what someone is saying. It is actively interacting with the individual, paying attention to what they are saying, and reacting to demonstrate we understand and appreciate their point of view.

Here are some pointers to help you improve your listening skills:

Being present: Being present is one of the most crucial things you can do while listening to someone. This includes putting aside distractions like your phone or computer and giving the individual your attention. Make eye contact, nod your head, and demonstrate your listening to the discourse.

Listen without passing judgment: When we listen with judgment, we often overlook essential nuances or fail to appreciate the other person's point of view. Instead, approach the topic with an open mind and listen without judgment. This will allow you to grasp the person's perspective better and create trust in the connection.

Paraphrase and clarify: To ensure that you comprehend the person's message accurately, explaining and paraphrasing what they are saying is critical. This entails paraphrasing what they've stated in your terms and asking clarifying questions.

Demonstrate empathy: Empathy is putting oneself in another person's shoes and comprehending their experiences and emotions. It's about being aware of their needs and experiences and reacting in a manner that demonstrates your concern. We'll go over this in greater depth later. Let us now go further into the topic of empathy.

Empathy is the capacity to comprehend and share another person's emotions. It's all about putting yourself in their shoes and viewing things through their eyes. When we demonstrate empathy, we establish a connection with the other person, which may aid in developing trust and strengthening relationships.

Here are some examples of how you might demonstrate empathy in your relationships with others:

Actively listening: Empathy cannot exist without active listening. When we actively listen, we demonstrate to the other person that we appreciate their viewpoint and wish to comprehend their thoughts and experiences.

Validate their emotions: Validating someone's sentiments is recognizing them and demonstrating that you understand their feelings. Saying things like, "I can see how that would be frustrating," or "That sounds difficult," may help.

Consider their experience: Reflecting on someone else's experience demonstrates that you understand how they feel and what they are going through. This might include stating, "It sounds like you're going through a difficult time," or "I can see how that would be difficult."

Avoid passing judgment or rejecting their emotions: We create a barrier to good communication when criticizing or discounting someone's sentiments. Instead, approach the topic with an open mind and notice their feelings without passing judgment.

Offer assistance: Assisting someone entails showing them that you care about them and are willing to assist them. This includes providing physical aid, emotional support, or listening.

In conclusion, good listening and empathy are essential components of successful communication. By actively listening and demonstrating empathy, we create an atmosphere where people feel heard, appreciated, and understood. It is critical to approach talks with an open mind, avoid judgment, and give assistance when necessary. Doing so strengthens our relationships, increases communication, and achieves more success in all aspects of our lives.

Giving and receiving feedback may be difficult, but it is necessary for personal and professional development. Feedback may assist you in identifying areas for growth as well as recognizing your abilities. However, criticism might be regarded as harmful, resulting in defensive and ineffective responses.

As a result, it is critical to address criticism constructively and honestly. This section will go over ways to offer and accept feedback efficiently.

Giving Feedback Techniques

Be specific and goal-oriented: It is critical to be detailed and impartial while providing comments. Use instances rather than generalizations to demonstrate your views. Objectivity guarantees that input is received as constructive rather than a personal assault.

Concentrate on Behaviors: Concentrate on the person's actions rather than their personality or character. This method decreases defensiveness while also ensuring that the criticism is actionable. Instead of stating, "You're a slacker," you may add, "I noticed you missed the deadline for the report."

Make use of "I" statements: Using "I" sentences decreases defensiveness while still communicating your sentiments and point of view. Instead of declaring, "You're doing it wrong," you may reply, "I'm having difficulty understanding your approach."

Suggestions for Improvement: Suggestions for improvement are essential for feedback to be useful. It assists the individual in understanding what they can do differently and how to make adjustments. Instead of stating, "You need to work harder," you may reply, "How about we break the task down into smaller pieces and set daily goals?"

Consider the Future: Feedback should be oriented toward the future rather than the past. Feedback is to assist the individual in improving and growing, not penalizing or condemning them. By focusing on the future, you can guarantee that the feedback is forward-thinking and useful.

Methods for Receiving Feedback

Be Mindful: Receiving feedback requires an open mind and a desire to learn. Avoid getting defensive or dismissive, even if the critique is difficult to hear. Instead, attempt to listen and comprehend the comments actively.

Clarification Questions: By asking clarifying questions, you can guarantee that you grasp the comments and how to improve. It also conveys to the donor that you respect their feedback and desire to learn from them. You may, for example, ask, "Can you give me an example of how I could improve in this area?"

Thank You to the Giver: Thanking the donor for their comments demonstrates that you respect their insight and viewpoint. It also motivates people to provide comments in the future. "Thank you for taking the time to provide feedback," for example. I appreciate your honesty and will strive to improve in this area."

Reflect on the Feedback: Thinking about the feedback assists you in comprehending it and figuring out how to better it. It also shows a development mentality and a desire to learn and progress. You may, for example, ask yourself, "What can I learn from this feedback?" "How can I improve using this information?"

Following up on comments displays your dedication to development and progress. It also demonstrates that you take comments seriously and are working to improve. For example, you may remark, "I've considered your feedback and made some changes." "Could you please give me more feedback on how I'm doing?"

Finally, offering and accepting feedback is necessary for personal and professional development. Following these strategies, feedback may be a constructive and beneficial instrument for self-improvement and goal achievement. Remember that feedback should be precise, objective, and behavior-focused.

HOW TO BE ASSERTIVE WITHOUT BEING AGGRESSIVE

The capacity to communicate your views, emotions, and wants in an open, honest, and courteous way without infringing the rights of others is referred to as assertiveness. It is an important ability that may help you communicate more effectively, create deeper relationships, and advocate for yourself in tough circumstances. Many individuals, however, conflate assertiveness with hostility and may avoid being forceful for fear of being viewed as impolite or aggressive.

Being forceful without being aggressive is feasible, but it takes an intentional effort to express oneself strongly but courteously. Here are some practical strategies to help you gain assertiveness without being aggressive:

Make use of "I" statements: It is critical to employ "I" statements rather than "you" statements when expressing your ideas or sentiments. Instead of criticizing or condemning the other person, communicate your unique experience and sentiments in this manner. Instead of stating, "You never listen to me," you may say, "I am frustrated when I am not heard."

Be particular and explicit: When making a request or expressing your demands, be specific and clear about what you desire. This reduces uncertainty and miscommunication, which may result in irritation and conflict. Instead of asking, "Can you assist me with this project?" you may ask, "Can you proofread this report and provide feedback by tomorrow at 3 PM?"

Active listening should be practiced: Listening is essential to good communication. Give someone your attention while speaking to you, and avoid interrupting or interjecting. When they have finished speaking, recap what they have said to verify that you have accurately understood them. Active listening demonstrates that you value the other person's viewpoint and contributes to developing trust and rapport.

Maintain a calm and courteous tone of speech: The tone of voice may transmit just as much meaning as the words themselves. Even if you are furious or disappointed, speak calmly and courteously. Avoid using strong words or yelling, which may exacerbate the issue and lead to confrontation.

Be receptive to feedback: Being forceful also entails being open to criticism and feedback. Avoid being defensive or dismissive while accepting comments. Instead, listen to the critique, ask clarifying questions, and think about how you might utilize it better. Establishing limits is an important element of being aggressive. It is about articulating your demands and limitations clearly and politely without infringing on the rights of others. Setting limits may help you avoid feelings of overload or resentment and develop stronger relationships.

Self-care is essential: Being assertive may be emotionally demanding, particularly if you are used to avoiding confrontation or repressing your emotions. Self-care may assist you in maintaining your emotional well-being and building resilience. Take pauses as required, participate in things that make you happy, and seek help from trustworthy friends or specialists if necessary.

To summarize, being assertive without being confrontational is an important ability that may help you communicate more effectively, develop deeper relationships, and advocate for yourself in tough circumstances. You may build firm and respectful assertiveness abilities by employing "I" statements, being explicit and detailed, practicing active listening, adopting a calm and polite tone, being receptive to criticism, establishing boundaries, and practicing self-care. You may grow more confident in expressing your views, emotions, and demands with practice and achieve better success in your personal and professional life.

TECHNIQUES FOR SETTLING DISPUTES AND HAVING PRODUCTIVE CONVERSATIONS IN CHALLENGING CIRCUMSTANCES

Conflict is an unavoidable aspect of life, and it may occur in any situation, including the workplace, personal relationships, and even inside oneself. Conflict, although unpleasant, may provide a chance for development and transformation. However, how you manage it may make or break you. Effective communication is essential for conflict resolution, and this part will go over six and a half ways to talk successfully in tough circumstances.

Listening Actively

Active listening is a strategy for understanding and remembering what is being said. It demands the listener to focus entirely on the speaker and provide a response that signals comprehension, such as nodding or summarizing. Active listening helps create trust and respect in a discourse when dealing with disputes. When we feel heard and understood, we are more inclined to be receptive to new ideas and solutions.

Maintain Your Cool

It is normal to feel emotionally heated in stressful circumstances. However, it is critical to remain cool and collected. Anger, irritation, and other strong emotions may distort our judgment and make effective communication difficult. Take a few calm breaths and concentrate on the topic rather than the emotions it has evoked.

Make use of "I" statements.

Accepting responsibility for your emotions and ideas while speaking in a quarrel is critical. Using "I" words rather than "you" statements allows you to express yourself without criticizing or assaulting the other person. Instead of stating, "You're always so selfish," you may respond, "I'm hurt when I don't feel like my needs are being met."

Demonstrate Sympathy

Empathy is the capacity to comprehend and share another person's emotions. When coping with a problem, showing empathy may assist in reducing tension and foster a feeling of connection among the persons involved. It demonstrates that you are open to seeing things from the other person's point of view and that you regard their sentiments.

Explain and summarize

Misunderstandings are common in communication, particularly during disagreements. Explaining and recapping what has been discussed is critical to guarantee that all sides are on the same page. This ensures that everyone is on the same page and demonstrates that you are listening and trying to understand.

Look for Solutions

When dealing with disagreement, it is critical to concentrate on finding a solution rather than merely expressing the issue. Brainstorming ideas with others may be an excellent technique to generate new solutions that benefit both sides. Remember that the aim is not to "win" the debate but to find a solution that fits the requirements of all parties involved.

Take a Rest

When emotions are running high, stepping away from the discussion may be important. This enables both parties to calm down and think about the situation before returning to it. It is critical to agree on a definite time to restart the talk and not to leave the problem unresolved for too long.

Finally, although disagreements may be difficult, they can also give chances for development and connection. You may communicate effectively and settle issues well and flexibly using these six-and-a-half tactics. Remember that conflict resolution is a talent that can be honed through practice and patience. You may become a great communicator who can easily handle challenging circumstances with time and effort.

THE SIGNIFICANCE OF EMOTIONAL INTELLIGENCE AND ITS UNDERSTANDING

Emotional intelligence is the capacity to detect and comprehend one's own emotions as well as the emotions of others and to utilize that knowledge to guide one's conduct and relationships. Emotional intelligence is becoming more crucial in today's fast-paced world, as it assists people in navigating difficult social circumstances, strengthening relationships, and achieving success in both personal and professional settings.

Emotional intelligence comprises two fundamental competencies: personal competence and social competence. Personal competence is defined as the capacity to detect and regulate one's emotions, and social competence is defined as the ability to comprehend and navigate the emotions of others. Let us look more closely at these talents and why they are significant.

Personal Competence

Self-awareness, self-regulation, and motivation are all components of personal competency. Self-awareness is the capacity to identify and comprehend one's emotions and how they influence behavior and decision-making. It entails being honest with oneself and admitting one's strengths and faults. The capacity to govern one's emotions and impulses and adapt to changing situations is called self-regulation. Maintaining a happy attitude, being focused on goals, and avoiding negative habits such as procrastination or impulsiveness are all part of it. Motivation is the capacity to channel one's emotions in a good direction and utilize them to propel oneself to success and accomplishment. It entails creating goals, taking initiative, and being tenacious in adversity.

Social Competence

Empathy, social skills, and relationship management are all components of social competency. The capacity to comprehend and connect to the feelings of others is referred to as empathy. It entails carefully listening, being aware of nonverbal signs, and displaying compassion and empathy.

Social skill is the capacity to speak effectively, develop relationships, and influence people. It entails reading a situation and adapting one's communication approach appropriately. Relationship management is the capacity to develop and sustain good relationships with people. It entails overcoming disagreements, collaborating, and handling unpleasant talks.

Why Does Emotional Intelligence Matter?

Emotional intelligence is essential for a variety of reasons. It, first and foremost, assists people in developing closer relationships with others. Understanding and connecting to people's emotions allows us to communicate more effectively, develop trust, and encourage collaboration. This is particularly true in the workplace, where cooperation and teamwork are critical to success.

Individuals with high emotional intelligence can handle stress and deal with adversity better. Understanding and controlling our emotions makes us more prepared to cope with obstacles and failures. This is especially critical in high-pressure situations, when being cool and focused may make the difference between success and failure.

Finally, emotional intelligence is critical for personal development and progress. When we can understand and regulate our emotions, we can better evaluate our strengths and flaws and take action to develop ourselves. This results in improved self-awareness, self-confidence, and a feeling of purpose and direction in life.

Finally, emotional intelligence is a vital talent becoming more relevant in today's fast-paced environment. We may strengthen our relationships, handle stress and tough circumstances, and achieve personal and professional success by strengthening our personal and social competence. It is a life-long endeavor, but well worth the effort.

Emotional intelligence relies heavily on self-awareness and self-regulation. When we are self-aware, we have a good awareness of our ideas, emotions, and actions. This comprehension enables us to recognize our strengths and shortcomings and make educated choices consistent with our beliefs and aspirations. Conversely, self-regulation refers to our capacity to govern our emotions and behavior in an acceptable and effective manner.

Several approaches may be used to promote self-awareness and self-regulation. Let's look at a few of them below:

Mindfulness Meditation: Mindfulness meditation entails paying attention to the current moment without judgment. This technique may help us become more aware of our thoughts, emotions, and bodily sensations, which can help us enhance our self-awareness. We may begin to detect patterns and triggers that impact our behavior as we become more conscious of these elements of ourselves. We can more successfully manage our emotions and conduct this way.

Journaling: Journaling is another helpful approach to increasing self-awareness. Writing down our emotions and ideas might assist us in identifying patterns and triggers that impact our behavior. It may also assist us in clarifying our beliefs and ambitions. We may become more self-aware and make better choices that match our beliefs and goals by frequently reflecting on our experiences and feelings.

Feedback: Seeking feedback from others is an effective technique to increase self-awareness. By soliciting feedback from others, we may obtain insight into how our conduct is seen and affects others. These comments may assist us in identifying flaws and areas for development.

Mindful Breathing: Mindful breathing is a strategy that entails concentrating on our breath and paying attention to our body's feelings. By soothing our nervous system and lowering tension, this exercise may help us control our emotions. We may become more aware of our emotions and control them more efficiently by adopting mindful Breathing into our everyday practice.

Self Reflection: Self-reflection is a practice that includes reflecting on our ideas, emotions, and actions. This exercise may help us understand our motives and ideals. We may become more self-aware and make better choices that align with our beliefs and goals by frequently reflecting on our experiences.

Gratitude Practice: Gratitude is a strong feeling that may aid with self-regulation. We may create a more optimistic outlook and better manage our emotions by concentrating on the good parts of our lives. We may become more self-aware and regulate our emotions more successfully by including a daily thankfulness practice into our routine.

Physical Exercise: Another excellent strategy for enhancing self-regulation is physical exercise. Endorphins are released during exercise, which may help alleviate stress and control our moods. We may improve our self-awareness and emotional management by including regular exercise.

By adopting these approaches, we may increase our self-awareness and self-regulation, which will help us make better judgments, improve our relationships, and accomplish our goals. It is vital to highlight that increasing self-awareness and self-regulation is a continual process that needs constant effort and dedication. However, adopting these tactics into our everyday routine may create a deeper self-awareness and help us manage our emotions more successfully.

Finally, self-awareness and self-regulation are important components of emotional intelligence and play an important role in human growth and development. We may increase our self-awareness and self-regulation by employing strategies like mindfulness meditation, Journaling, feedback, mindful Breathing, self-reflection, gratitude practice, and physical activity. These approaches can help us accomplish our goals and live a more satisfying life.

TECHNIQUES FOR ENHANCING SOCIAL SKILLS AND EMPATHY

Empathy and social skills are essential for forming strong bonds and connecting with people. People with great empathetic talents frequently understand and connect to others on a deeper level, making communicating and forming meaningful relationships simpler. This part will look at numerous ways to develop empathy and social skills. These tactics can help you become a better listener, connect with people more effectively, and develop greater relationships.

Active listening: Active listening is the practice of carefully listening to what others say and reacting accordingly. It entails staying in the moment, avoiding distractions, and concentrating on the speaker. Begin by keeping eye contact, nodding and confirming, and summarizing what the speaker has said to demonstrate that you have comprehended their message.

Learn to understand body language: Even if a person isn't saying anything, their body language may indicate a lot about their feelings. Understanding body language may help you detect and react appropriately when someone is sad, uncomfortable, or furious. Pay attention to facial expressions, gestures, and posture, and let this influence your replies.

Practice Empathy: Empathy entails putting oneself in another person's shoes and attempting to comprehend their point of view. When you develop empathy, you improve your ability to connect to people and react sympathetically and helpfully. Begin by listening carefully and asking open-ended questions to understand the person's experience better.

Improve your communication skills: More than speaking clearly and articulately is required for effective communication. It also entails active listening, empathy, and proper response. To convey your sentiments, use "I" statements rather than "you" statements, and avoid making assumptions about what others think or feel. Building great relationships takes time, and it demands patience and effort. Be kind to yourself and others as you go through the process of connecting and developing social skills.

Volunteer: Volunteering is an excellent approach to developing empathy and social skills. It helps you to engage with individuals from other backgrounds and have a better understanding of their perspectives. Volunteering also allows for developing skills such as active listening, effective communication, and empathy.

Seek feedback: Feedback might help you improve your social skills. Seek input from others on how you seem in social settings, and utilize this knowledge to make changes and improvements.

Take social risks: To build meaningful relationships, you must be willing to take chances and put yourself out there.

Attending social gatherings, starting discussions, and reaching out to people may be part of this. While it might be frightening, taking social risks is important in establishing social skills and successful relationships.

Practice Mindfulness: Mindfulness is the discipline of being present in the present moment without judgment. Mindfulness practice may help you become more aware of your thoughts and emotions, improving your capacity to connect with people and react properly.

Participate in a social skills group: Individuals may practice social skills and create relationships in a safe and supportive atmosphere via social skills groups. Structured activities and exercises aimed to enhance empathy, active listening, effective communication, and other social skills are frequently included in these groups.

Developing empathy and social skills takes time and effort, but they are critical for developing good relationships and connecting with people. You may acquire the abilities to form healthy relationships and achieve personal and professional success by practicing active listening, learning to interpret body language, exercising empathy, developing effective communication skills, and taking social risks.

Life is full of obstacles and disappointments; our resilience is determined by how we react to them. Resiliency is the capacity to bounce back from hardship and retain a positive view in the face of adversity. It is an important part of personal development and necessary for everybody who wants to attain their goals.

Here are some ways to build resilience and recover from setbacks:

Self-care is essential

Self-care is vital for sustaining excellent physical and mental health, which is required for resilience development. Regular exercise, proper food, and enough sleep help you retain a positive mentality and manage stress more successfully.

Create a strong support network

When developing resilience, having a strong support network may make all the difference. When times are tough, reach out to friends and family members on whom you can depend for emotional support and encouragement.

Create a growth attitude

A growth mindset is the concept that you can improve your talents and intellect through hard effort, commitment, and persistence. Adopting a growth mindset may help you perceive setbacks as opportunities for development and learning rather than failures.

Practice mindfulness

Mindfulness is a valuable technique for stress management and resilience development. You may learn to regulate your thoughts and emotions more efficiently and build a stronger feeling of inner peace and tranquility by practicing mindfulness practices such as deep breathing, meditation, and yoga.

Set attainable goals

Setting attainable goals helps save you from being overwhelmed and frustrated by failures. Break major ambitions into smaller, more manageable stages, and celebrate each tiny win.

Failure teaches us valuable lessons

Failure is an unavoidable aspect of life, and learning from failure is important to developing resilience. Rather than obsessing over your faults, use this time to consider what went wrong and what you can do better next time.

Develop an optimistic attitude

Maintaining a positive attitude is critical for developing resilience. Concentrate on the good things in your life and attempt to reinterpret unfavorable events as chances for development and learning.

Seek expert assistance if necessary

If you are experiencing stress, anxiety, or other mental health issues, don't be afraid to seek professional assistance. A skilled therapist can provide the skills and support you need to overcome setbacks and develop resilience.

Finally, cultivating resilience is important for attaining personal development and success. You can develop the resilience you need to bounce back from setbacks and achieve your goals by practicing self-care, cultivating a positive mindset, developing a growth mindset, practicing mindfulness, setting realistic goals, learning from failure, cultivating a positive mindset, and seeking professional help if necessary.

Life is full of ups and downs, and we all face difficult circumstances that may lead to stress and overwhelm. Learning how to handle stress and emotions is critical for sustaining our emotional and physical well-being, whether it's a challenging job assignment, a relationship difficulty, or a health condition. Here are some pointers on dealing with stress and emotions in difficult situations:

Practice Mindfulness

Mindfulness is a strategy that entails being completely present and engaged in the present moment without judgment. We are better equipped to handle stress and control our emotions when we are aware. Mindfulness may be practiced via meditation, deep breathing, or just spending a few seconds concentrating on your surroundings. You may acquire insight into your responses and learn to respond more efficiently by focusing on your thoughts and feelings.

Determine Your Triggers

Understanding what causes stress and bad emotions is a vital first step in dealing with them. Attempt to recognize circumstances, people, or events that cause tension, anxiety, or other unpleasant feelings. Once you've discovered your triggers, you may take action to avoid or better manage them. For example, if you know that a specific person or event consistently creates tension, you may plan ahead of time or avoid the situation entirely.

Make Use of Positive Self-Talk

The way we communicate with ourselves has a big influence on our emotions and stress levels. Negative self-talk may cause worry, self-doubt, and overload, while good self-talk can keep us calm and focused. Instead of telling yourself you can't manage a problem, consider reframing it as a task you can conquer. Positive affirmations help you create confidence and remain motivated.

Exercise regularly

Exercise is an excellent strategy to reduce stress and improve your mood. Endorphins, which are natural mood enhancers, are released during physical exercise. Exercise also aids in the reduction of muscular tension and the promotion of relaxation. Even a brief stroll or stretching might help reduce tension and relax your thoughts.

Practice Gratitude

Focusing on your blessings might help you adjust your perspective and lessen stress. Spend a few minutes each day reflecting on the things in your life for which you are grateful. This might be anything from a helpful buddy to a stunning sunset. Gratitude fosters pleasant feelings and improves resilience in the face of adversity.

Take breaks and care for yourself.

When faced with difficult conditions, it is tempting to disregard our needs. However, taking breaks and practicing self-care are critical for managing stress and emotions. Spend time doing activities that make you happy, such as bathing, reading a book, or spending time with loved ones. Make rest a priority to avoid burnout.

Seek Assistance

When you need assistance, don't be hesitant to ask for it. A support system may help you manage stress and emotions, whether talking to a friend or seeking professional therapy. Talking to someone might help you gain perspective and discover fresh answers to your problems.

Laugh

Laughter is an excellent stress reliever. Endorphins are released, muscular tension is reduced, and mood is improved. Watch a hilarious film or television program, read a funny book, or spend time with individuals who make you laugh. Laughter is an excellent stress reliever and promoter of general well-being.

Finally, regulating stress and emotions is critical for preserving our mental and physical health. We may successfully handle stress and emotions in difficult circumstances by practicing mindfulness, recognizing triggers, utilizing positive self-talk, exercising frequently, practicing gratitude, pausing, self-care, finding assistance, and laughing.

CHAPTER 8: DEVELOPING A SUPPORT SYSTEM AND FOSTERING RELATIONSHIPS

THE VALUE OF ESTABLISHING AND MAINTAINING STRONG RELATIONSHIPS

Building and sustaining strong relationships is essential to personal development and success. Relationships may take numerous forms, including those with family, friends, coworkers, and acquaintances. We have a support system to turn to in times of need, someone to share our joys and achievements with, and people who can give vital criticism and advice when we have good relationships.

On the other hand, building and sustaining good relationships may be difficult, particularly in today's fast-paced and digitally linked society. Despite having many social media followers and virtual relationships, many individuals feel isolated and lonely. Building and sustaining meaningful relationships involves time, effort, and a willingness to be vulnerable and real.

Here are some of the reasons why developing and sustaining healthy relationships is critical for personal development:

Relationships provide a person with a feeling of belonging and connection.

Humans are social beings that want connection and a feeling of belonging. We feel connected to people and purpose and belonging when establishing good relationships. This bond may make us happier, more satisfied, and less lonely.

Emotional support is provided via relationships

Having a support system may be useful when we confront tough times or circumstances. Strong relationships may provide emotional support, whether a shoulder to weep on, a listening ear, or encouraging words. Emotional support may help us negotiate life's ups and downs and recover from setbacks.

Personal development possibilities are provided via relationships

Strong relationships also provide chances for personal development. We may learn and develop from others with various viewpoints, experiences, and ideas when we surround ourselves with them. Strong relationships may push us to stretch our boundaries, try new things, and become better versions of ourselves.

Accountability is provided via relationships

We have individuals who can keep us responsible when we have good ties. This accountability is valuable in helping us achieve our goals and change our lives. We are more inclined to push ourselves and strive for excellence when we have individuals who believe in us and our abilities.

Now that we know how important it is to create and maintain great relationships let's look at some techniques for doing so:

Be present and attentive

Being present and attentive to people is one of the most essential parts of developing successful relationships. This entails putting aside distractions like phones and computers and focusing completely on the person we are with. Being present and attentive demonstrates that we regard the other person and contributes to developing trust and connection.

Be vulnerable and genuine

Strong partnerships need vulnerability and sincerity. When we are vulnerable, we generate deeper relationships and trust and share our challenges, concerns, and dreams with others. Authenticity is also important in developing strong relationships. We attract individuals who share our ideals and appreciate us for who we are when we are honest with ourselves and our principles.

Effective communication is essential

Building and sustaining successful relationships requires effective communication. This entails actively listening, clearly and politely expressing oneself and being receptive to criticism. We may prevent misunderstandings and develop stronger relationships with people when we communicate properly.

Make time for relationships

It takes time and effort to build and sustain strong relationships. In our hectic lives, it is critical to prioritize relationships and make time for them. Setting aside time for relationships indicates that we respect them and helps deepen them over time, whether via frequent phone conversations, coffee dates, or trips.

Finally, healthy relationships are crucial for personal development and success. A feeling of belonging and connection, emotional support, opportunity for personal development, and responsibility are all provided by strong relationships.

We may establish and sustain good relationships that last a lifetime by being present and attentive, vulnerable and real, speaking effectively, and making time for relationships.

METHODS FOR ESTABLISHING RAPPORT AND TRUST WITH PEOPLE

Building rapport and trust with people is essential for effective communication and relationships. Rapport is the feeling of mutual understanding and connection that develops between people. Trust is the trust or faith that one has in the dependability, integrity, and competency of another. Communication may break down without rapport and trust, relationships collapse, and goals become unattainable.

Fortunately, you may use several practical ways to establish rapport and trust with people. Here are a few of the most effective:

Listening actively: Active listening is one of the most crucial skills for developing rapport and trust with people. Active listening is giving complete attention to what the other person is saying, asking pertinent questions, and demonstrating empathy and comprehension. When you actively listen to someone, you show that you appreciate their ideas and perspectives and offer a safe atmosphere for open and honest discussion.

Nonverbal communication: Nonverbal communication consists of Body language, facial expressions, and tone of voice. Because it can transmit feelings and attitudes that words cannot, it is a strong instrument for creating rapport and trust. For example, a grin, nod, or eye contact might show friendliness and openness, but crossed arms or a scowl can imply defensiveness or indifference.

Authenticity: The technique of being truthful to oneself and others is called authenticity. It entails expressing yourself honestly and freely without attempting to be someone you are not. When you are honest, you demonstrate that you are real and trustworthy, which builds trust.

Common Ground: Finding common ground with individuals is another powerful approach for establishing rapport and trust. This entails recognizing mutual interests, values, or experiences you have with the other individual. Finding common ground fosters connection and understanding, which may lead to deeper relationships.

Positive attitude: Maintaining a good attitude is vital for developing rapport and trust with people. A good attitude entails being upbeat, helpful, and encouraging. It may generate infectious excitement and energy, as well as aid in the development of mutual respect and trust.

Empathy: Empathy is the capacity to comprehend and share another person's emotions. It entails putting oneself in their shoes and seeing the scenario from their eyes. When you display empathy, you indicate that you care about the other person's emotions and problems and build trust and rapport.

Open-mindedness: Open-mindedness entails being sensitive to new ideas, opinions, and experiences. It may aid in developing trust and rapport by demonstrating a desire to learn and grow and creating a feeling of mutual respect and understanding.

Consistency: Consistency is essential when it comes to establishing rapport and trust with people. It entails following through on your obligations, being trustworthy, and acting consistently. When you are consistent, you display dependability, trustworthiness, mutual respect, and trust.

Communication skills: Effective communication abilities are required to develop rapport and trust with people. This is part of using clear and simple language, being polite and kind, and avoiding misunderstandings or misinterpretations. Good communication skills assist in developing trust and rapport by ensuring that communications are presented clearly and responsibly.

Finally, following up with people is crucial for developing rapport and trust. Following up with the other person after a meeting, chat, or encounter may cement the connection and indicate your dedication to creating trust and rapport.

Finally, developing rapport and trust with people is critical for effective communication and relationships.

TIPS ON HOW TO COMMUNICATE WELL IN BOTH PERSONAL AND PROFESSIONAL SETTINGS

Effective communication is essential for developing strong and healthy professional and personal relationships. Communication is not just speaking and communicating your message but also listening and comprehending the other person's point of view. In this part, we will review some effective communication methods to help you create greater relationships with others.

Be concise and clear

Communication requires clarity. It is important to communicate clearly and succinctly while talking with people. Avoid employing unclear terms. Jargon is a language that the other person may not comprehend. Use simple language to minimize confusion or misunderstandings and convey your views and emotions.

Pay Close Attention

Listening is an essential component of good communication. When someone is speaking to you, you must give them your full attention. Try to refrain from interrupting or completing their statements. Instead, pay close attention to what they're saying and answer accordingly. Active listening may help you grasp the other person's point of view while also building trust and connection.

Avoid Making Assumptions

Assuming the other person's thoughts or feelings may lead to misunderstandings and disputes. Instead of forming assumptions, ask clarifying questions to clear up any uncertainties or uncertainty. Avoid leaping to conclusions before gathering all of the data.

Differences must be respected

Everyone has their own set of views, values, and ideas. It is important to appreciate these differences and refrain from judging or condemning people based on their views or principles. By accepting diversity, you can create a safe and inclusive atmosphere where everyone feels valued and appreciated.

Make Use of Nonverbal Communication

Nonverbal communication may transmit a great deal of information without using words. Your tone of speech, facial expressions, and body language may all convey your emotions and ideas. Make sure your nonverbal communication matches your vocal communication. For example, if you say "yes" but shake your head, the other person may be confused or believe you are not telling the truth.

Avoid blaming or accusing others

Accusing or blaming people might elicit defensive or angry reactions. Instead of blaming, convey your thoughts and needs using "I" phrases. Instead of stating, "You never listen to me," try, "I feel ignored when talking to you."

Empathy should be practiced

Empathy is the capacity to comprehend and share the emotions of others. When speaking with people, put yourself in their shoes and try to comprehend their point of view. Empathy may aid in developing better relationships and creating a more pleasant and supportive atmosphere.

Request Feedback

Requesting feedback helps you understand how people see you and your communication style. It may also assist you in identifying areas for improvement. When soliciting feedback, be open to constructive criticism and utilize it to enhance your communication abilities.

Use Positive Reinforcement.

Good reinforcement may drive and promote good conduct in others. When someone communicates effectively or achieves your expectations, give them good comments to encourage them to keep doing so.

Avoid passing judgment

Judgments may be damaging and provoke defensive or angry reactions. Rather than judging or condemning others, concentrate on the conduct or circumstance at hand. Use terms that indicate blame or criticism sparingly, such as "you always" or "you never."

Good communication is a crucial ability that may assist you in developing closer relationships with others. By following these guidelines, you may enhance your communication skills and create a good and supportive atmosphere in both personal and professional interactions. Remember to be clear and concise, listen carefully, avoid assumptions, accept differences, utilize nonverbal communication, avoid blaming or accusations, exercise empathy, ask for feedback, use positive reinforcement, and avoid passing judgment. You may improve your communication skills and develop healthier relationships with practice and determination.

Relationships may provide us happiness, pleasure, and progress but can also bring us tension, suffering, and toxicity. Toxic relationships may take many different forms and can be difficult to detect and manage. This section will look at how to recognize toxic relationships, their effects on our lives, and effective ways to handle them.

Detecting Toxic Relationships

Toxic relationships exhibit behaviors that jeopardize your well-being, self-esteem, and feeling of safety. Here are some warning indicators that you are in a toxic relationship:

Constant Criticism: If your spouse or acquaintance always criticizes and puts you down, it may indicate a poisonous relationship. Constant criticism may undermine your self-esteem and make you feel you are never good enough.

Controlling Behaviors: If your spouse or companion is always attempting to exert control over you and your activities, it may indicate a poisonous relationship. Controlling habits makes you feel like you don't have control over your life, limiting your potential to develop and prosper.

Verbal or physical abuse: If your spouse or a friend is verbally or physically abusive to you, it is an indication of a poisonous relationship. Abuse may be detrimental to your emotional and physical health, leaving you feeling lonely and alone.

Lack of Trust: If your spouse or friend is continually questioning your motivations, accusing you of cheating or lying, or checking up on you, it might be an indication of a toxic relationship. A lack of trust may corrode your relationship's basis and make it harder to sustain a strong connection.

One-sided Relationships: If your spouse or friend always takes from you and provides nothing in return, this might indicate a toxic relationship. One-sided relationships may leave you feeling unloved, devalued, and emotionally depleted.

The Dangers of Toxic Relationships

Toxic relationships may have serious consequences for your emotional and physical health, as well as your general well-being. Here are some of the ways toxic relationships may affect your life:

Depression and Anxiety: Chronic stress from toxic relationships may lead to anxiety and despair. Constant criticism, control, and abuse may make you feel imprisoned and helpless, resulting in emotions of hopelessness and despair.

Self-esteem is low: Toxic relationships may destroy your self-esteem, making you feel inadequate and unworthy of love and respect. This might result in emotions of embarrassment, remorse, and self-doubt.

Isolation: Toxic relationships may make you feel isolated and alone because your spouse or friend may attempt to isolate you from your support system, including friends and family.

Physical Health Issues: Chronic stress from toxic relationships may cause physical health difficulties, including headaches, intestinal problems, and chronic discomfort.

Self-Destructive Behaviors: Some persons may engage in self-destructive behaviors such as drug addiction or self-harm to deal with the stress of a toxic relationship.

Toxic Relationship Management

If you have discovered that you are in a toxic relationship, you must take effective action to manage it. Here are some techniques that may be useful:

Establish Limits: Setting boundaries is essential in dealing with unhealthy relationships. Tell your spouse or acquaintance what actions are unacceptable and establish your limits.

Seek Help: Seek assistance from friends, relatives, or a therapist. Speaking with someone who understands might make you feel less alone and more powerful.

Focus on Self-Care: Take care of yourself by doing things that make you happy and relaxed.

TECHNIQUES FOR CREATING A NETWORK OF SUPPORT AND REQUESTING ASSISTANCE WHEN NECESSARY

It is commonly believed that we should be self-sufficient, independent, and capable of dealing with things independently. This perspective, however, may be destructive to our well-being, personal progress, and success. Building a support network and asking for assistance when required is important for personal growth and reaching our goals.

Here are eight and a half methods for developing a support network and soliciting assistance when needed:

Recognize the importance of a support network

We are social animals that need social ties to survive. Creating a support network may help us overcome difficulties and accomplish our goals by providing emotional support, practical guidance, and resources. Recognizing the value of a support network is the first step in creating one.

Identify possible sources of assistance

Creating a support network begins with identifying possible sources of assistance. Friends, family members, coworkers, mentors, coaches, therapists, or support groups may all be included. Consider the individuals in your life who are encouraging, supportive, and capable of providing the assistance you need.

Determine the kind of assistance you need

It is critical to be clear about the kind of assistance you need. Communicating your requirements to your support network may help them deliver the correct care, whether you need emotional support, practical counsel, or resources.

Be ready to reciprocate

Creating a support network is a two-way street, and you must be prepared to reciprocate. Be accessible to give assistance when your support network needs it, and be willing to assist when appropriate.

Develop your relationships gradually

Building relationships takes time, and it is critical to do it gradually. Begin by reaching out to prospective sources of assistance and establishing rapport. Relationships may be progressively deepened and trust built as they grow.

Join organizations and groups

Joining clubs and organizations may be a great way to expand your support network. Joining a group with common interests, whether a recreational club, a professional organization, or a volunteer group, may allow for meeting like-minded individuals and creating relationships.

Be open to new opportunities

Creating a support network necessitates being open to new relationships. Be willing to meet new people and form relationships with them. You never know where your next source of assistance will come from.

Practice being vulnerable and real

Creating a support network requires being vulnerable and real. Being honest about your issues, difficulties, and requirements is critical. When you practice vulnerability and honesty, you open the door for people to connect with you on a deeper level and give you the support you need.

Don't be hesitant to seek assistance

The most crucial approach for developing a support network is not to be scared to ask for assistance. Asking for assistance may be difficult, particularly if you are used to being self-sufficient. However, seeking assistance is a show of strength, not weakness. When you ask for help, you open the door for others to give the assistance you need to attain your goals.

In conclusion, developing a support network and seeking assistance when required are critical components of personal development and attaining our goals. You can build a support network that will help you achieve your full potential by recognizing the importance of a support network, identifying potential sources of support, being clear about what kind of support you need, being willing to reciprocate, gradually building relationships, joining groups and organizations, being open to new relationships, practicing vulnerability and authenticity, and not being afraid to ask for help.

Understanding your present financial condition and defining financial goals are critical to personal development and self-improvement. Setting and attaining financial goals may help you achieve financial security and independence, which are essential to a satisfying life.

To begin, it is critical to understand your existing financial condition. This entails closely scrutinizing your income, spending, assets, and obligations. A simple balance sheet is created by listing all your assets, such as bank accounts, investments, and property, and subtracting your obligations, such as credit card debt, loans, and mortgages. This will provide you with an accurate view of your net worth.

You may begin creating financial goals after you understand your present financial condition. These goals must be specific, measurable, attainable, relevant, and time-bound (SMART). Instead of expressing "I want to save money," a SMART goal might be "I want to save $5,000 in the next 12 months by reducing discretionary spending and increasing my income through a side hustle."

When creating financial goals, it is important to consider both short-term and long-term goals. Paying off debt, saving for a trip, or establishing an emergency fund are all examples of short-term goals. Long-term goals include saving for retirement, purchasing a home, or establishing a company.

It is critical to have a strategy in place to attain your financial goals. This entails breaking down your ambitions into smaller, more manageable tasks. For example, suppose you want to pay off credit card debt. In that case, you may devise a strategy that involves paying more than the minimum monthly payment, reducing discretionary spending, and looking for methods to boost your income.

It's also critical to keep track of your financial success. This might help you remain motivated and make necessary changes to your strategy. You may keep track of your progress by utilizing a spreadsheet, a budgeting tool, or just writing it down in a diary.

Good money habits are another crucial component of planning and accomplishing financial goals. This involves making a budget, living within your means, and avoiding debt to the greatest extent feasible. Investing in your financial education by reading books, attending seminars, and getting financial guidance from specialists is also critical.

In addition to personal financial goals, you should think about your long-term financial future. These are all examples of retirement planning, estate planning, and insurance planning. Retirement planning includes putting money aside for retirement via employer-sponsored plans like 401(k)s and IRAs, as well as personal savings and investments. Estate planning is devising a strategy for your possessions after your death, including creating a will and trust. Insurance planning entails safeguarding your assets and yourself via different forms of insurance, such as life insurance, health insurance, and disability insurance.

To summarize, evaluating your financial condition and defining financial goals are critical to personal development and self-improvement. You may attain financial stability and independence by setting SMART goals, breaking them down into doable stages, and building good money habits.

Investing in your financial knowledge and preparing for your long-term financial future via retirement, estate, and insurance planning is also critical.

DEVELOPING A SPENDING PLAN AND MONITORING COSTS

Budgeting and monitoring spending are critical components of financial planning and wealth growth. A budget may assist you in understanding your income and costs, prioritizing your spending, and saving for future goals. Managing your money properly and attaining financial stability without a budget might be difficult. In this part, we'll go over how to make a budget, manage your spending, and apply these skills to attain financial success.

Making a Budget:

Understanding your income and spending is the first step in creating a budget. To construct a budget, compile your financial information, such as your income, bills, and other spending. The first stage is to compute your net income, which is your earnings after taxes and other deductions. This amount will serve as the foundation for your budget.

Following that, you must make a list of your costs. Begin by noting your fixed costs, which are recurrent monthly expenses such as rent or mortgage payments, auto payments, and insurance fees.

Next, include your variable costs: monthly spending on food, entertainment, and clothes.

It's time to balance your budget once you've recorded your income and spending. To establish if you have a surplus or a deficit:

1. Subtract your costs from your revenue.

2. If you have extra money, consider putting it into savings or investing.

3. If you have a deficit, consider reducing your spending or raising your revenue.

Keeping track of spending:

Keeping track of your spending is an important element of budgeting. You may uncover areas where you can reduce spending and save money by monitoring your costs. There are various methods for keeping track of your costs, including budgeting applications, spreadsheets, and pen and paper.

It's critical to be careful and precise while documenting your costs. Keep track of all your spending, including tiny items like coffee or snacks. These minor purchases may easily mount up and wreck your budget. Tracking everything allows you to discover areas where you're overpaying and make changes to remain on budget.

Making the Most of Your Money:

Making a budget and keeping track of your spending are simply the first steps. The secret to financial success is making smart financial choices utilizing your budget. Your budget should direct your spending, assist you in prioritizing your costs, and make it simpler for you to save money.

Setting financial goals is one method to make use of your money. Your budget helps you identify areas where you can reduce spending and redirect that money toward your financial goals. For example, if you want to pay off debt, you may direct excess cash toward that purpose.

Making educated financial choices is another approach to utilizing your budget. When purchasing, check your budget to verify whether you have enough money. If you don't, try deferring the purchase until you have the finances or search for areas where you can cut down on spending.

Finally, your budget should be updated regularly. Your budget should evolve in tandem with your income and spending.

Review and alter your budget frequently to ensure you're on track.

Finally, making a budget and monitoring costs is critical to financial success. You can make educated financial choices, prioritize your spending, and save for future goals if you understand your income and costs. Remember to keep detailed and accurate expenditure records, utilize your budget to guide your spending, and make sound financial choices. Using these techniques, you may attain financial stability and establish a secure financial future.

MONEY-SAVING AND WEALTH-BUILDING TECHNIQUES

Saving money and building wealth over time is important to personal development and financial security. You may use various ways to optimize your savings and grow wealth, whether you are saving for a down payment on a house, creating an emergency fund, or preparing for retirement.

Create a budget: Making a budget is the first step in saving money and generating wealth. A budget allows you to identify your income and spending while providing a structure for managing your money. To construct a budget, list all your income and spending, including fixed costs such as rent and utilities, variable expenses such as food and entertainment, and discretionary expenses such as dining out and shopping. You may find areas where you can cut down and shift those dollars to savings and investments after you comprehensively grasp your income and spending.

Automate your savings: Saving money automatically is a terrific method to make it a habit. Set up frequent automatic transfers from your checking account to your savings or investment account, such as weekly or monthly. You won't have to remember to transfer money every time, and you'll be less inclined to waste it.

Use cash-back credit cards: Cash-back credit cards are a great way to earn money on ordinary transactions. Look for credit cards with significant cash-back incentives for grocery, petrol, and restaurants. To prevent interest costs, make these purchases using your credit card and pay them off each month.

Think of a high-yield savings account: A high-yield savings account is a form of savings account that pays a greater interest rate than other types of savings accounts. Look for a high-yield savings account at a bank or credit union and compare rates to discover the best choice. Remember that some accounts may have a higher minimum balance requirement or other limitations.

Invest in a retirement account: Investing in a retirement account, such as a 401(k) or an IRA, is a terrific way to grow long-term wealth. These accounts give tax benefits and may produce compound interest over time. Contribute enough to obtain the full company match if your workplace provides a 401(k) plan. Consider starting an IRA if you don't have access to a 401(k) plan.

Maximize your employer's benefits: Many organizations provide other benefits in addition to 401(k) plans, such as health savings accounts (HSAs) and flexible spending accounts (FSAs). Make the most of these perks to save money on healthcare and other qualified costs.

Pay off high-interest debt: Before accumulating wealth, pay off high-interest debt, such as credit card debt or personal loans. High-interest debt may greatly impede saving and growing wealth since interest costs can rapidly add up. Make a strategy to pay off high-interest debt as soon as possible, and consider consolidating debt with a balance transfer credit card or personal loan to minimize interest rates.

Consider investing in real estate: Investing in real estate may be a terrific method to create wealth over time. To diversify your portfolio and develop long-term wealth, consider investing in rental properties, flipping homes, or real estate investment trusts (REITs).

Save for large purchases:

1. If you have a large purchase coming up, such as a new automobile or a home renovation, start saving for it now.

2. Make a savings goal and a strategy to save a certain amount each month.

3. Consider opening a separate savings account or creating a sinking fund to save for these items.

Keep track of your progress: Finally, it is critical to track your success as you save and develop money. Establish frequent checkpoints for reviewing your budget, savings, and investments and adjusting your strategy as required.

LONG-TERM FINANCIAL GROWTH INVESTING TECHNIQUES

Investing is a critical component of long-term financial success. You might make larger returns on your money by investing it instead of standard savings accounts or other low-risk investments. However, investing has its own set of hazards, and navigating the world of investments without sufficient education and assistance may be difficult. This part will look at some of the most popular long-term financial growth investment techniques.

Diversification

The strategy of investing in a range of assets to lessen the risk of losing money is known as diversification. You could lessen the effect of market volatility on your portfolio by diversifying your assets across multiple sectors, industries, and asset classes. A well-diversified portfolio may include stocks, bonds, mutual funds, ETFs, real estate, and other alternative assets.

Dollar-cost averaging

Dollar-cost averaging is investing a predetermined sum at regular periods, independent of market circumstances. This technique enables you to purchase more shares when the market is low and fewer shares when the market is high, thus decreasing the effect of market swings on your portfolio.

Buy-and-hold

The buy-and-hold strategy is a long-term investing strategy that involves purchasing stocks or other assets and keeping them for a prolonged time, often several years or more. This technique is based on the premise that the stock market rises over time and that short-term volatility is less relevant than the long-term trend.

Value Investing

A value investing technique is purchasing undervalued companies or trading at a discount on their real worth. This method requires a thorough grasp of the company's core fundamentals, such as its financial statements, management team, and industry trends.

Growth investing

Growth investing is a technique that entails purchasing stocks of firms with the potential for rapid development in the future. This strategy focuses on firms with a significant competitive advantage, innovative goods or services, and an increasing market share.

Income investing

Income investing is a strategy that includes investing in assets that produce a consistent dividend, such as dividend-paying stocks, bonds, and real estate investment trusts (REITs). This strategy is popular among retirees and others looking for a consistent source of income from their assets.

Indexes investing

Index investing is a technique that entails investing in a portfolio of stocks or other assets that correspond to a certain market index, such as the S&P 500 or the Dow Jones Industrial Average. This strategy gives wide market exposure and may cost less than actively managed funds.

Socially responsible investment

SRI (socially responsible investment) is a method that includes investing in firms that fulfill specific ethical or environmental standards. In addition to financial success, this method evaluates the effect of the company's activities on society and the environment.

Alternative investments

Alternative investments are non-traditional assets that may provide more diversity and better returns than typical investments. Private equity, hedge funds, commodities, and real estate are examples of alternative investments.

Robo-advisors

Online financial platforms that employ algorithms and computer models to give investment advice and manage portfolios are known as robo-advisors. This technique may provide cheaper costs than typical financial consultants and may be a viable alternative for folks just starting to invest.

Finally, there are several investment options for long-term financial gain. Before selecting a strategy that works for you, you must establish your investing goals, risk tolerance, and time horizon. A well-diversified portfolio of stocks, bonds, and alternative assets may provide the greatest opportunity for long-term financial success.

Before making any investing choices, always speak with a financial adviser.

TIPS FOR REACHING FINANCIAL SECURITY AND MAKING RETIREMENT PLANS

Financial independence and retirement planning are essential components of human development and self-improvement. Financial independence is the capacity to sustain oneself without depending on others or being linked to a certain employment or source of money. Retirement planning is developing and executing a financial strategy to allow you to live well in retirement. Here are some suggestions for financial freedom and retirement preparation.

Set financial goals

Setting financial goals is the first step toward financial freedom and retirement planning. Specific, measurable, achievable, relevant, and time-bound goals (SMART) are recommended. Determine how much you need to save when you want to retire and your desired lifestyle. Create an action plan to reach your financial goals once established.

Live within your means

Living within your means is an important part of achieving financial freedom. Avoid living paycheck to paycheck by saving at least 20% of your salary. Make and stick to a budget, and eliminate needless spending. Avoid taking up debt and pay off any existing debt as soon as feasible.

Invest in Retirement Accounts

Investing in retirement accounts is a critical step in retirement planning. Utilize tax-advantaged retirement accounts such as 401(k)s, IRAs, and Roth IRAs. Contribute as much as possible, and gradually raise your payments as your income rises.

Diversify Your Investments

Diversifying your assets may help you decrease risk while increasing your profits. Consider investing in a combination of stocks, bonds, and mutual funds and diversifying your assets across industries and asset classes. To maintain the correct asset allocation, rebalance your portfolio regularly.

Reduce Taxes

Tax reduction allows you to retain more money and reach financial independence sooner. Utilize tax breaks and credits, and think about tax-efficient investment techniques such as tax-loss harvesting and tax-deferred annuities.

Begin Saving Early

Beginning to save early will significantly improve your potential to attain financial independence and prepare for retirement. The sooner you start saving, the longer your money has to grow. Use compounding interest to your advantage and prevent procrastination.

Avoid High Fees

Avoiding exorbitant fees may optimize your earnings and reach financial freedom sooner. Avoid high-fee mutual funds and investment consultants in favor of low-cost investing choices such as index funds and exchange-traded funds (ETFs).

Consider a Side Hustle

Consider beginning a side venture to supplement your income and hasten your journey to financial freedom. Look for ways to monetize your talents and hobbies by freelancing, consulting, or launching a small company.

Safeguard Yourself and Your Assets

Protecting yourself and your possessions is critical for financial independence and retirement planning. Purchase sufficient insurance coverage, such as health insurance, disability insurance, and life insurance. Consider establishing a trust or other estate planning options to safeguard your assets and save taxes.

Seek Professional Help

Seeking expert assistance may help you make educated financial choices and achieve your financial goals. Consider hiring a financial planner or adviser specializing in retirement and investment management. Look for someone who is a fiduciary looking out for your best interests.

To summarize, financial independence and retirement planning need a mix of discipline, patience, and educated decision-making. You can achieve financial independence and plan for a comfortable retirement by setting specific financial goals, living within your means, investing in retirement accounts, diversifying your investments, minimizing taxes, starting to save early, avoiding high fees, considering a side hustle, protecting yourself and your assets, and seeking professional advice.

Chapter 10: Techniques for Mindfulness and Meditation for Inner Calm and Peace

RECOGNIZING THE ADVANTAGES OF MEDITATION AND MINDFULNESS

In recent years, mindfulness and meditation have grown in popularity, with many individuals turning to these techniques to relieve stress, worry, and other unpleasant feelings. While mindfulness and meditation may seem to be new-age fads, they originated in old spiritual traditions and have been practiced for millennia. In this part, we will look at the advantages of mindfulness and meditation and their impact on mental, emotional, and physical health.

First, it is critical to recognize that mindfulness and meditation are not synonymous. While the terms are often used interchangeably, they represent separate activities with distinct goals. Mindfulness is the discipline of being fully present at the moment, without judgment or distraction. At the same time, meditation is the deliberate concentration of the mind on a single object or activity, such as the breath or a mantra. Both approaches may be employed in conjunction or alone to produce comparable results.

The power of mindfulness and meditation to relieve stress and anxiety is one of its most important advantages. Regular mindfulness and meditation practice have been found in studies to lower cortisol, the stress hormone, and boost serotonin and dopamine levels, which are connected with well-being and pleasure. Mindfulness and meditation, by concentrating on the present moment and fostering nonjudgmental awareness, may help us let go of anxieties about the past or future, lowering stress and anxiety in the process.

Mindfulness, meditation, and stress reduction have been found to improve mental health. According to research, these techniques may help with depression and anxiety symptoms, increase attention and concentration, and even improve cognitive performance. We may build a stronger feeling of peace, clarity, and mental stability by training the mind to concentrate on the present moment, which can favor general mental health.

Mindfulness and meditation have been proven to improve physical and mental health. According to research, these habits may decrease blood pressure, boost immunological function, and even cut the risk of heart disease. Mindfulness and meditation may increase the body's natural healing processes by lowering stress and encouraging relaxation, resulting in greater health and well-being.

Finally, it has been shown that mindfulness and meditation have tremendous impacts on spiritual well-being. These practices may help us connect with our inner selves and the world by building a better feeling of mindfulness and nonjudgmental presence. Mindfulness and meditation are a way to spiritual development and personal change for many individuals, helping build a stronger sense of meaning, purpose, and connection.

Finally, the advantages of mindfulness and meditation are extensive, including mental, emotional, physical, and spiritual well-being. Whether you want to decrease stress, improve mental health, improve physical health, or connect with your inner self, mindfulness and meditation may be effective techniques. By adopting these practices into your everyday routine, you may experience the transformational impact of mindfulness and meditation in your own life.

Mindfulness practice in everyday life is critical for gaining inner serenity and tranquility. It is a means of focusing on whatever activity we do in the present moment without judgment or distraction.

Mindfulness cannot be learned immediately; it takes time and effort. In this part, we'll look at various ways of fostering awareness in everyday life.

Mindful Breathing

Mindful breathing is a method that requires attention to the breath and is one of the most basic mindfulness techniques. Find a quiet spot and sit or lie down in a comfortable posture to practice mindful breathing. Close your eyes and take a few deep breaths, then return your attention to breathing. Take note of the sensations of air entering and exiting your body. Notice how your chest and belly rise and fall with each inhale and exhale. If your thoughts stray, gently bring them back to your breath.

Mindful Eating

Mindful eating is a strategy that includes paying attention to one's eating experience. To practice mindful eating, choose a small quantity of food and consume it in a calm, distraction-free environment. Take a few long breaths to center yourself, then concentrate on the meal. Take note of the food's colors, textures, and tastes. Chew gently and relish each meal, paying attention to your tongue and throat sensations. Be mindful of how the food affects you both physically and emotionally.

Mindful walking

Mindful walking is a strategy that entails walking slowly and purposefully while paying attention to the sensation of walking. Find a quiet spot to stroll where you won't be bothered to practice mindful walking. Begin walking gently and pay attention to how your feet feel on the ground. Take note of how your legs move and your weight shifts with each stride. Pay attention to the sights, sounds, and fragrances around you.

Body Scan Meditation

Body scan meditation is a practice that entails concentrating on various regions of the body and paying attention to the physical sensations in each place. Close your eyes and lie down in a comfortable position to practice body scan meditation. Beginning at the top of your head, concentrate on each area of your body one at a time. Any bodily feelings, such as tension, warmth, or tingling, should be noted. If your mind wanders, gently bring it back to the portion of the body you're concentrating on.

Mindful bathing

Mindful bathing is a practice that includes paying attention to the showering experience. Shower in a calm, distraction-free environment to practice mindful showering. Take note of how the water feels on your skin, the temperature, and the sound. Take note of the soap's or shampoo's aroma and texture. Be mindful of the ideas and feelings that occur throughout your shower.

Mindful cleaning

Mindful cleaning is a strategy that includes paying attention to the cleaning process. Choose a small area to clean and concentrate on the work to practice mindful cleaning. As you clean, pay attention to the texture and aroma of the cleaning solution, the sound of the brush or sponge, and the feel of your hands. Be mindful of your thoughts and emotions while you clean.

Mindful listening

Mindful listening is a practice in which you pay close attention to the noises around you. Find a quiet spot and sit or stand comfortably to practice mindful listening. Close your eyes and concentrate on the noises around you. Take note of the level and quality of each sound, as well as any ideas or feelings that come while you listen.

Meditation is a great technique for cultivating inner peace and tranquility in your everyday life. It has been used for ages to relieve stress, improve attention, and promote general well-being. On the other hand, starting a meditation practice may be tough, and making it a habit can be much more difficult. In this part, we'll review some practical advice for meditation and making it a habit.

Begin small

When beginning a meditation practice, it is critical to begin slowly. Begin with a few minutes daily and progressively increase the duration as you gain confidence in the exercise. Trying to meditate for a long time might be stressful and frustrating, making it more difficult to become a habit.

Find a peaceful and comfortable location

Meditation is best conducted in a peaceful, comfortable, and distraction-free atmosphere. Find an area where you will not be bothered and feel comfortable and quiet. This may be a spare room, a park, or even a nook in your bedroom.

Use a guided meditation

Guided meditations may be a valuable resource for individuals new to meditation. They serve as a foundation for your practice and might assist you in remaining focused and calm. Several guided meditations are accessible online, so try them all until you discover one that speaks to you.

Focus on your breath

Focusing on your breath is one of the most basic and effective meditation practices. Close your eyes and take slow, deep breaths, focusing on the feeling of air going in and out of your body. If your mind wanders, softly return your attention to your breathing.

Be consistent

When it comes to developing a meditation practice, consistency is essential. Make meditation a non-negotiable component of your daily routine by setting out a specified period each day. Find a time that works for you and stick to it, whether first thing in the morning or before bed.

Use a timer

When beginning a meditation practice, using a timer might be beneficial. Set a timer for the duration of your meditation, and don't stop until the timer goes off. This will help you concentrate and keep you from continuously checking the time.

Don't be too hard on yourself

Beginners often believe they are not doing it correctly or that their minds are too occupied to focus. Remember that meditation is a skill that takes time to master. Be kind to yourself and refrain from criticizing your experience. Instead, concentrate on the procedure and the advantages you are experiencing.

Experiment with various approaches

There are several meditation methods to select, so try them all until you discover one that works. Some prefer mantra meditation, while others prefer awareness or visualization. Experiment with several ways until you discover one that works for you.

Participate in a group

Meditation groups may be an excellent way to keep you inspired and engaged in your practice. Look for local meditation groups or join an online community in your region.

Being a member of a group may bring accountability and support.

Celebrate your accomplishments

Finally, remember to rejoice in your accomplishments. Every time you meditate, you deepen your practice and create a habit. Don't berate yourself if you miss a day or two. Instead, concentrate on your efforts to include meditation in your daily routine.

To summarize, beginning a meditation practice might be difficult, but it is well worth the effort. You may build a regular meditation practice that can help you cultivate inner peace and tranquility by beginning simply, finding a peaceful and comfortable sitting area, and being consistent.

MINDFULNESS EXERCISES FOR MANAGING STRESS AND EMOTIONS

The practice of concentrating on the present moment with nonjudgmental awareness is known as mindfulness. It is an effective technique for stress reduction and emotional regulation since it helps you build a feeling of serenity and inner peace amid everyday bustle. In this part, we'll look at several mindfulness activities you may implement to manage stress and emotions in your everyday routine.

Body Scan Meditation: Body scan meditation is a mindfulness technique that includes deliberately concentrating on various areas of your body, from your toes to the top of your head. As you concentrate on each body component, you bring your attention to any feelings, tensions, or discomfort you may be feeling. This technique may assist you in tuning into your body and releasing any physical tension or stress you may be carrying.

Find a comfortable location to sit or lie down to begin the body scan meditation. To focus yourself, close your eyes and take a few deep breaths. Begin by paying attention to your toes. Notify yourself of any feelings or tensions in your toes, and then gradually shift your attention up your body, concentrating on each body component. Take your time with each body area, and try to approach any sensations with curiosity and nonjudgmental awareness.

Mindful breathing: Mindful breathing is a simple yet effective mindfulness exercise that may help you manage stress and control your emotions. It entails concentrating your attention on your breathing, observing the feelings of each inhale and exhale without judgment or distraction.
Find a quiet spot where you may sit comfortably to practice mindful breathing. To focus yourself, close your eyes and take a few deep breaths. Then, begin to concentrate on your breathing. Take note of the feeling of air entering and leaving your nose, the rise and fall of your chest or abdomen, and the duration and rhythm of each breath. If your thoughts stray, gently return them to your breath without judgment or impatience.

Loving-Kindness Meditation: Loving-kindness meditation is a mindfulness practice in which you cultivate sentiments of love, kindness, and compassion for yourself and others. It may aid in the development of resilience, the reduction of stress, and the enhancement of emotions of connection and well-being.

Find a peaceful spot where you may sit comfortably to practice loving-kindness meditation. To focus yourself, close your eyes and take a few deep breaths. Then, think about someone you care about profoundly, such as a close friend or family member.

Imagine them and quietly repeat the following sentences in your mind: "May you be happy. May you have a long and healthy life. May you stay safe. "May you find peace." Repeat these sentences multiple times, paying attention to the sensations of love and compassion that occur.

Next, consider someone you have no feelings for, such as a coworker or an acquaintance. Rep these sentences for this individual, concentrating on creating sentiments of love and compassion for them.

Finally, consider someone you disagree with, such as a tough colleague or family member. Repeat the same lines for this individual, acknowledging that they are entitled to happiness, health, safety, and tranquility.

Mindful Walking: Mindful walking is a mindfulness exercise that includes concentrating your attention on the physical sensations of walking, such as foot movement, breath rhythm, and the sights and sounds around you. Even in the middle of a hectic day, it may help you build a feeling of calm and concentration.

Find a quiet spot to stroll comfortably and securely to practice mindful walking. To center yourself, start by standing motionless and taking a few deep breaths. Then, start walking slowly and attentively, paying attention to each stride and feeling in your body.

HOW TO INCLUDE MINDFULNESS AND MEDITATION INTO YOUR PATH TOWARD GENERAL SELF-IMPROVEMENT

Mindfulness and meditation are effective techniques for achieving inner peace, reducing stress and anxiety, and improving general well-being. However, incorporating these practices into your everyday routine might be difficult, particularly if you are new.

This part will look at practical suggestions and ways to include mindfulness and meditation into your entire self-improvement path.

Begin small: When beginning a new habit, it is critical to begin small and gradually build up. This method applies to mindfulness and meditation techniques. Begin by devoting only a few minutes daily to your practice and progressively expand the time as you gain confidence.

Create a routine: Making mindfulness and meditation a habit requires consistency. Create a routine by allocating a definite time each day for your practice. This might be done in the morning, during a lunch break, or before bed.

Make a separate area: Making a separate location for your mindfulness and meditation practice will help you understand the correct frame of mind. Choose a pleasant and quiet location where you may sit comfortably and without interruptions.

Guided meditations are an excellent way to get started with your meditation practice. Several applications and websites provide guided meditations of varying durations and subjects. Choose one that speaks to you and use it to guide your practice.

Be present: Being mindful is all about being present in the moment. Focus on your breath, bodily sensations, or a specific object or mantra while practicing mindfulness and meditation. When your thoughts stray, gently draw them back to the current moment.

Practice self-compassion: During meditation, it is normal for your mind to wander and ideas and emotions to emerge. Rather than condemning yourself or becoming irritated, practice self-compassion. Be nice and kind to yourself, and remember that meditation is a practice, not an achievement.

Use mindfulness in everyday activities: Mindfulness does not have to be restricted to meditation. You may integrate mindfulness into regular activities like eating, walking, and housework. Concentrate on the current moment and include your senses in the task.

Join a community: Mindfulness and meditation may be solitary practices, but they do not have to be. Joining a community of like-minded people may give you support, encouragement, and inspiration to keep up your practice.

Be patient: Integrating mindfulness and meditation into your routine requires time and perseverance, like any new habit. Expect no instant results or changes. Instead, concentrate on the task and enjoy the ride.

Experiment with several techniques: There are many different mindfulness and meditation approaches, and what works for one person may not work for another. Experiment with several ways to discover what works for you and what you appreciate.

Including mindfulness and meditation in your self-improvement path may be a life-changing experience. It may assist you in cultivating inner peace, improving general well-being, and reducing stress and worry. However, it is important to remember that mindfulness and meditation are disciplines that, like any other, need time and patience to develop. You may incorporate mindfulness and meditation into your everyday routine and get the advantages by beginning small, developing a pattern, and practicing self-compassion.

This section will discuss the extraordinary success stories of eighteen sports, entertainment, and other superstars. These eighteen great people overcame hardship to become world-renowned. I am convinced that their stories will inspire and encourage you. So, let us delve into these exceptional people's interesting journeys.

1. Sylvester Stallone

Sylvester Stallone's success story is one of the most inspirational. He was practically a starving artist before he became famous. He performed odd jobs to pay the bills for many years throughout and after his undergraduate years. And he'd do it all while taking on whatever acting gigs he could get to keep his ambitions of being a successful actor alive.

It was a battle Stallone would fight for many years, seven. Throughout those seven trying years, he would earn a few minor parts in a few films. But none of them were magnificent enough to begin his career.

During those seven long years of struggle, he came close to poverty. At one time, Stallone was so desperate for cash that he had to sell his wife's jewels. He had to sell his dog since he couldn't feed it. Stallone's situation deteriorated to the point that he was forced to live on the streets for a brief period.

However, his days as an aspiring actor would not endure forever. After fighting insurmountable difficulties for almost seven years, he eventually received his big break. And this break would come after he managed to get a screenplay he penned in three days of inspiration in front of two big-name Hollywood directors.

This crucial event would be decisive for Sylvester Stallone. His career would take off once he landed the starring part in the film known as "Rocky."

Success finally comes to those who have always wished for it.

2. Oprah Winfrey

Oprah Winfrey's success story is one-of-a-kind. She faced difficulties and poverty at a young age that most people would find difficult to overcome. In rural Mississippi, she was born into poverty and a shattered household. Her parents, who were just 18 and 19 when she was born, divorced shortly after. This resulted in her grandmother taking her in.

Her grandma, on the other hand, was not your normal warm and fluffy grandmother. No, she was a tough-talking grandma who was a strict disciplinarian who punished her for little infractions. However, the poverty and controlled lifestyle did not endure long, as she returned to her mother at the age of six.

Oprah would later endure sexual abuse at a young age, having been assaulted by some of her family members as young as nine. She soon began engaging in exceedingly dangerous activities after being emotionally abandoned, abused, and assaulted. Her actions led to her being pregnant at the age of fourteen.

Her mother then booted her out of the home since she became pregnant. Oprah went on to live with her father, only to lose the baby a week after birth.

Oprah's childhood was fraught with suffering and tragedy. Regardless of her tragic experiences, she vowed to change her life when she lost her kid. So, she resolved to earn an education, do her best, and pursue her aspirations.

She resolved to begin trusting herself again, to love herself, and to make decisions that would enrich her life rather than ruin it. She eventually gained enough confidence to compete in a beauty competition. Her involvement in this pageant would later lead to a career as a radio station newscaster.

Oprah's love of speaking in front of an audience laid the groundwork for her future success as a news anchor. She used to host a TV chat show in Maryland, leading to her morning talk show in Chicago.

And the rest, as they say, is history. Oprah overcame enormous obstacles in her childhood. These are challenges that put far too many people on the sidelines. She opted to transform her wounds into knowledge, and she became one of the most successful talk show hosts in history (while also inspiring many others to do the same) with her self-titled talk program, The Oprah Winfrey Show. Oprah is currently one of America's wealthiest self-made women.

3. Arnold Schwarzenegger

We wouldn't dare to remove Arnold Schwarzenegger from our collection of success stories since he is the ideal of the self-made man. Arnold was born in Austria and reared there. He grew up when the country was still reeling from World War II loss.

Alcoholism was widespread, defeatism was the norm, and grandiose dreams were scorned in his surroundings. The odds were stacked against Arnold.

Arnold, on the other hand, was unconcerned. He knew he did not want to live the typical Austrian life his parents desired. He also knew he wanted to migrate to America since it was the land of the free, so he devised a strategy to become a bodybuilding success. Then, I will use that accomplishment to break into the film industry. And, indeed, he did precisely that. He realized his objective by being the youngest man to win a Mr. Universe competition, five Mr. Universe titles, and seven Mr. Olympia championships.

After accomplishing his bodybuilding goals, he pursued the acting profession he had always desired. And, indeed, he would go on to dominate the film business to the same extent that he had won the bodybuilding world. He featured in many blockbuster films that grossed over $3 billion, earning him one of Hollywood's largest net worths.

4. J.K. Rowling

J.K. Rowling had a childhood goal of becoming a writer. However, she would have to persevere for many years before her ambition of being a published novelist came true. Her mother's death would derail her efforts to put her thoughts for her book on paper almost as soon as she chose to begin.

Rowling sought employment as a teacher in another nation to avoid the ensuing downturn. Soon after, she married and had a kid, further delaying her ambitions.

Rowling's marriage would collapse suddenly only one year after it started, but things weren't over for her. This resulted in her being unemployed with a kid and barely living on unemployment benefits.

Despite her difficulties, Rowling will continue to work on her novel. And she did it by writing during every free time her kid was sleeping until the day she finished her novel.

Of course, even after Rowling completed her novel, challenges persisted. Twelve different publishers rejected her book. The rejection crushed her emotions, and she was on the verge of quitting. Fortunately, she gave it another shot. And it was at that very time when J.K. Rowling's fortunes improved. She eventually found a publisher that would take her work.

J.K. Rowling has since become one of the best-selling writers of all time. She is also the world's highest-paid author. Her works have been translated into over 80 languages and have sold over 600 million copies. Persistence and patience pay off in the long term.

5. Steven Spielberg

Most people are unaware that Steven Spielberg was rejected three times from film school. But he didn't give up, and he applied repeatedly until he was approved. Cal State Long Beach eventually accepted him into their film department.

Fortunately for Spielberg, he was able to use his experience at Cal State to get an unpaid internship at Universal Studios.

Of course, this internship wouldn't continue forever. Still, it was long enough for him to learn how to sneak into the studios unnoticed to constantly acquire information on what it took to succeed in the field.

Finally, the day would arrive when he could get a film he had written into the hands of Hollywood executives. But first, he had to fight the film bosses' repeated efforts to convince him to quit.

After being repeatedly warned that the film size was incorrect and rebuilding the whole demo to the suggested sizes, the executives ultimately relented and offered him a chance with his film. The film went on to win several honors, cementing Steven Spielberg's status in the business.

Steven Spielberg is currently regarded as one of the most influential filmmakers ever. In addition, he is currently one of the richest. And, like all of our inspiring success stories, his experience demonstrates that if you knock long and hard enough, the doors of opportunity will finally swing open for you.

6. Mary Kay Ash

Mary Kay Ash's success story is encouraging. She was born in a tiny Texas town, married, and had a family at 17. She had three children with her husband, who was in the military but finally divorced.

Mary Kay would struggle for years to care for her children alone. However, she took on numerous sales roles in the direct selling profession and worked her way up the corporate ladder.

However, after many years of selling numerous goods and a few middle management and trainer jobs, she began to feel ignored for the more important leadership roles she desired due to her gender. As a result, she resolved to take things into her own hands.

Mary Kay Ash, 45, wanted to start her own business when her children were grown and on their own. As a result, she established her own cosmetics firm. She began small, but in a few short years, she transformed Mary Kay Cosmetics into a multi-billion-dollar organization that today serves and inspires individuals all over the globe.

Despite being beyond what most people consider her prime, Mary Kay went on to write many best-selling books, including The Mary Kay Way, Miracles Happen, and You Can Have It All, among others. She became an inspiration to countless women. As a result of her company's success and her desire to inspire as many people as possible, she became a multimillionaire. She was ultimately dubbed "The Greatest Woman In American History."

7. Cristiano Ronaldo

Cristiano Ronaldo was raised in a low-income home. As a youngster, he had to share a room with three of his brothers because of their poor financial status. There were even instances when they couldn't afford to purchase a soccer ball so he could play in the streets. But Ronaldo did not allow his surroundings to determine his fate.

No, he'd find methods to enjoy his favorite sport even without a ball. He'd build a makeshift ball out of bottles, rags, or whatever he could find just so he could play.

Cristiano would eventually become so good at soccer that, at 11, he would have to make the ultimate sacrifice by moving almost 500 miles away from his home to train at a prominent soccer school. It's a good thing he did, too, since he set himself up to become one of the greatest players in history.

The Portuguese Football Federation has named Cristiano Ronaldo the best Portuguese footballer ever. Millions of soccer fans throughout the world consider him to be the best of all time.

In addition, he is the first soccer player in history to earn more than $1 billion and has one of the highest net worths among professional athletes.

8. Lionel Messi

While talking about soccer, we can't leave out Lionel Messi's success story, which is just as amazing. Here's why, at the age of 11, Messi was kicked off his soccer squad because he was too little. He was little, but that was because he lacked growth hormone, making him much smaller than the other youngsters his age.

Fortunately, Messi was not discouraged. Instead, he would put himself on a rigid regimen in which he would inject himself with growth hormones. He would then inject himself with this hormone for seven days in one leg, followed by seven days in the other. Messi would maintain this regimen for the next six years.

The good news is that Messi's effort and perseverance paid off. He is now one of the highest-paid soccer players, with a tremendous net worth, and is regarded by legions of fans as one of the greatest soccer players of all time, having won soccer's top honor, 'The Ballon d'Or,' eight times.

Success requires sacrifice.

9. Michael Jordan

We can't talk about the best of all time in soccer without mentioning the guy many regard as the greatest in basketball. Most people are unaware that Michael Jordan had tremendous goals of being a great basketball player when he was only a sophomore in high school.

So, he took a risk and tried out for the Varsity squad. However, his coaches dismissed him from the squad. They didn't perceive his worth and didn't believe he was ready.

This rejection particularly hurt Jordan because of his lofty goals and ambitions. The rejection affected him so badly that he went home and sobbed in his closet.

Jordan brushed himself up and went all in for the JV squad, even though the rejection still pained him. He trained like no other throughout the offseason and gained four inches. He tried out for the varsity squad again the following year. But he succeeded the second time.

He made it and became the team's MVP, made the All-American Team, and won a college scholarship. And you already know the rest of the story.

Michael Jordan became the guy who scored 32,292 points in his basketball career. Jordan became the first person to win six NBA titles. The guy who also won five MVP awards and is widely regarded as the best basketball player ever.

Among all the success stories we've explored, this one demonstrates the value of having high expectations and being resilient in the face of rejection.

10. Paulo Coelho

Over 30 years ago, a book called 'The Alchemist' was released with little fanfare. The author of this book, Paulo Coelho, was informed by the first retailer who carried his book that just one person purchased a copy after it was published. Despite hearing the dismal findings, Coelho remained confident in his job.

Paulo Coelho waited for better outcomes. Unfortunately, he had to wait six months before selling his second copy. Surprisingly, the person who purchased his first book was also the one who purchased his second.

After the first year, the publisher determined that the book failed and terminated Coelho's contract. Fortunately, Coelho was able to overcome his early loss. He was determined not to give up, so he pursued his goal more vigorously by finding another publisher.

"Now, Coelho has found a new publisher, but it has not been easy, as he has faced rejection after rejection." But, after many rejections, he eventually got that new publisher and another chance to realize his ambition with it.

Coelho's aspirations began to come true from that point forward. He initially barely sold three thousand books.

However, sales continued to come in. And as time passed, he would sell ten thousand, then a hundred thousand, and so on.

Coelho's luck has yet to run out, as his book sales continue to rise year after year, with over 150 million copies of 'The Alchemist' sold to date. Even more astounding, he sold over 320 million books when all his other works were included. But it all began with the first book!

Paulo Coelho's success story demonstrates that if you sincerely want something, the world will conspire to help you accomplish the impossible.

11. President Abraham Lincoln

Most of us are familiar with this remarkable guy because of his work for enslaved individuals in the United States of America. He issued the Emancipation Proclamation, a monumental achievement that resulted in the end of slavery.

Most people don't recognize that Abraham Lincoln has one of the most amazing track records when it comes to conquering adversity.

His success narrative consists of a lengthy record of failures and setbacks that would surprise even one of the most accomplished and respected presidents of the United States of America.

Here's an excellent illustration of Lincoln's numerous failures, with a few triumphs thrown in for good measure:

- 1832: Lost his job
- 1832: Defeated for legislature
- 1833: Failed in business
- 1834: Elected to legislature
- 1835: The woman he loved died
- 1836: Had a nervous breakdown
- 1838: Defeated for Speaker
- 1843: Defeated for nomination for Congress
- 1848: Lost re-nomination
- 1849: Reject for Land Officer
- 1854: Defeated for Senate
- 1856: Defeated for nomination for Vice-President
- 1858: Again defeated for Senate
- 1860: Elected for President of The United States of America

To be true, Lincoln almost failed his way to success, and his documented failures help us comprehend the truth behind the Michael Jordan adage we stated earlier: failure is the road to success.

This success story, in particular, should persuade you that just because you haven't yet succeeded in life doesn't imply you never will. So, keep pushing and prepare for your big day; it will come if you keep your eye on the goal and keep going ahead.

12. Tom Brady

Tom Brady is one of our favorite inspiring success stories. Brady did not enter the NFL via the traditional athletic route. While most players begin training for the sport in third grade, Tom Brady would not step on the field until ninth grade.

His first appearance on the football field did not occur until his sophomore year. His chance came when the JV team's starting quarterback resigned. Fortunately for Brady, that chance helped him secure the starting Varsity QB position at the start of his Junior year.

Brady would become a Michigan Wolverine after achieving excellence in high school. At this level, however, Brady's success was not certain. No, he had to work for it.

Brady entered the program as the underdog, with seven quarterbacks ahead of him on the depth chart. Brady's tenacity finally landed him the desired starting position by the time he was a Junior, despite almost asking for a transfer to another school.

Brady would have further challenges in the pros. Brady was determined to play in the pros but had little interest in the draft. He was taken as the 199th selection in the sixth round, barely making it into the league.

Almost every coach in the league severely misjudged and undervalued Brady. His draft report from the 2000 NFL Draft listed the following characteristics:

- Poor Build | Skinny
- Lacks Great Physical Stature and Strength
- Lacks Mobility and Ability to Avoid The Rush
- Lacks a Really Strong Arm
- Can't Drive The Ball Down Field
- Doesn't Throw a Really Tight Spiral
- System-Type Player Who Can Get Exposed if Forced to Adlib
- Easily Knocked Down

Remember, Tom Brady was not the top-ranked quarterback, the finest athlete, or the best groomed for the sport. Furthermore, he did not have the finest stats or mechanics. Tom Brady, on the other hand, had the greatest heart and drive.

Thus, through sheer willpower, he pushed himself to become one of the greatest football players ever. And he has proved his case with the following accolades:

- Most NFL Championships by a Player (7x)
- Most Games Won by a Quarterback
- Most Games Played by a Quarterback
- Most Combined Passing Yards
- Most Touchdown Passes
- Most 4th Quarter Comebacks
- Best Touchdown to Interception Ratio
- 5 Time Super Bowl MVP
- 3 Time MVP of the NFL
- 2 Time NFL All-Decade Team Player
- Only Player to Win a Super Bowl for Both The AFC & NFC

13. Sarah Blakely

This success story is about Sarah Blakely, who Forbes named as one of the world's youngest self-made millionaires. Her narrative starts with her liking the firm appearance of pantyhose but despising how they appeared with open-toe shoes.

Blakely's aversion to pantyhose led to her constantly cutting the foot off of her pantyhose to get the desired appearance. She had a lightbulb moment after observing that many other ladies were doing the same thing. And she began to consider developing a solution that would answer this issue.

After viewing an exciting Oprah broadcast one day, Sarah decided to take big action on her concept. So she put everything on the line by spending her whole $5,000 life savings to go to Atlanta, GA. She planned to begin mass manufacturing of her product concept as she arrived.

Blakely first encountered a great deal of opposition. Nobody wanted to make the product she was attempting to develop. They decided it was too dangerous and a waste of time. Her patent officer hesitated to take her proposal seriously, believing it to be a flop.

She eventually succeeded after two years of preparing, several late hours, and a lot of no's. Her break came when a manufacturer agreed to produce her wares. And when Neiman Marcus and Bloomingdales took a chance on her by stocking her items in their shops.

Her first year in the company brought in more than $4 million in sales. Every year following that, her sales increased significantly. Sarah's bravery in going all in and her determination to promote her concept to the public aided her in becoming a billionaire by the age of 41.

14. Grant Cardone

This following anecdote emphasizes that it is never too late to be who you might have been. It's also a nice reminder that you can change no matter where you come from or where you've been. It demonstrates that anybody can clean up their act and achieve great success.

This is the account of a guy who grew up impoverished in Louisiana, lost his father when he was young, and was raised in a single-parent family with four additional siblings. It's about a guy called Grant Cardone.

Cardone isn't your average celebrity. He didn't come from a wealthy family. He is not a Hollywood celebrity. He also has no extraordinary ability, such as scriptwriting, politics, or sports. However, what he does have is something we all have, which is a will to succeed.

In his youth, Grant Cardone was in poor company. He was engaged with and addicted to narcotics, and he had been on a downhill spiral for more than a decade. He ultimately resolved to alter his life after being robbed at gunpoint, beaten to a bloody pulp with a pistol, and then forced out of his mother's home.

Grant Cardone resolved to clean up his act when he was 25. He removed all harmful influences from his life, became sober, and accepted the first job he could find.

This was a job as a car salesman. It was a title and a position that Grant despised. Because the economy was sluggish, he didn't have many alternatives, so he made it work.

Cardone is committed to becoming the greatest salesman he can be. As a result, he substantially engaged in his self-improvement by reading books and researching his art and profession.

His salary rapidly increased after he committed to achieving his best. He will soon become one of the greatest automotive salesmen in the nation. He finally started his firm and was exceedingly wise and careful with his money.

Cardone spent money exclusively on what was essential for food and shelter. Anything left over would be put into a real estate investment fund.

Grant Cardone's emphasis on learning more to earn more and the discipline to spend his additional money instead of squandering it on frivolous things enabled him to become a self-made billionaire by 30, only five years later.

Cardone has become a well-known worldwide businessman, speaker, and the owner of Cardone Capital, a $1.5 billion investment company. He's written the New York Times bestselling books If You're Not First, You're Last, The 10X

Rule, and the Axiom Award-winning Sell or Be Sold. In addition, he established Cardone University, a prominent sales training website with over 50,000,000 members and counting.

Grant Cardone just needed five years to transform his life fully. Imagine what five years might accomplish for you if you had the appropriate mentality and a strong will.

15 Kevin Hart

Kevin Hart is well-known and popular. He's been making us laugh and amused for a long time. Most people don't realize that Kevin Hart had to overcome some huge challenges before becoming one of the world's most popular comedians.

Hart had to endure a tumultuous upbringing with a father who was irresponsible, destructive, and often making problems. For years, he had to face the difficulties of a two-hour commute.

Hart has to deal with critics regularly. Someone he admired in the profession advised him to give up comedy. Due to his performances, he had to endure booing, heckling, and having chicken wings thrown at him.

Kevin Hart had to overcome several obstacles to make a return. He had to make the decision not to quit again and again. He opted to keep fighting for his ambitions, ignoring the detractors, skeptics, and anybody who questioned them.

On the other hand, Hart's perseverance and dedication to his idea would pay off in the end. After years of job stagnation, rejection, and near-death experiences, the tide would shift for Kevin Hart.

Kevin Hart is currently regarded as one of the world's top ten comedians. He's also one of the wealthiest. So, if you believe you can't achieve anything, consider Kevin Hart's success story and all he went through. Because if he can accomplish it, you can as well.

16. Tony Robbins

Tony Robbins had a difficult childhood. His parents split when he was seven, and his mother remarried four times as he grew up.

Tony and his siblings were up in a tumultuous atmosphere because of his mother's unstable relationships with men. Robbins, the eldest of three siblings, felt forced to stand up and assist his family in coping in a home dominated by a substance-abusing mother.

Robbins had to mature quickly. As a teenager, he had to do the food shopping for the family every week since his mother couldn't be bothered. He also had to make everyone's meals since no one else would.

Robbins eventually had to work many jobs in his childhood simply to get the expenses covered. Surprisingly, Robbins would accomplish all this without a vehicle, depending only on public transit.

Robbins fell out with his mother when he was 17, and she booted him out of the home. He completed high school but did not attend college.

He suffered for a few years with just a high school graduation, performing menial jobs that sapped the life out of him. He gained weight, became bankrupt, and began to despair about his predicament.

After attending a Jim Rohn seminar, he was motivated to change his life. He accepted Rohn's message of optimism and the power of accepting responsibility for one's circumstances. He utilized that idea to approach Jim Rohn for employment, which Rohn gladly accepted.

Robbins quickly rose to prominence as one of Rohn's top salespeople. Robbins was so successful that he was a billionaire by age 26, just via sales.

Robbins finally broke out on his own and became the best-selling author, high-performance coach, and multimillionaire the world has come to know and love, leveraging everything he learned from Rohn.

The narrative of Tony Robbins demonstrates that our history does not equal our future. And you may overcome sluggish beginnings and difficult surroundings to live a full and great life.

17. Stephen King

Stephen King, an avid horror enthusiast, liked spine-chilling books. Nonetheless, his path to achievement was fraught with failures. Stephen King's career began as a high school English teacher. He endured several rejections from publishers while struggling to make finances meet. His breakthrough came when he sold "Carrie," a book he had thrown away out of despair. His wife rescued the manuscript from the garbage.

King sent the work to Doubleday with his wife's support, landing a publishing agreement that would transform his life forever. Since then, he has sold over 400 million books worldwide. King has written 65 novels, seven of which were published under Richard Bachman, and five non-fiction works. He has authored approximately 200 short stories, most appearing in book collections.

18. Jim Carrey

The story of Jim Carrey manifesting his aspirations is a stunning tribute to the power of imagination and steadfast self-belief. Carrey sent a check to himself for $10 million early in his career when he struggled to build a name for himself in Hollywood. He rescheduled it for Thanksgiving Day, 1995, and sent a message thanking him "for acting services rendered."

This cheque was kept in Carrey's wallet as a reminder of his objectives and aspirations. He'd often go up to the Hollywood Hills, sit in his vehicle, and fantasize about being a famous actor. While staring at that $10 million cheque, he envisioned directors applauding his work and people asking for signatures.

In what can only be characterized as a fateful twist of fate. His breakthrough came when he was selected as a regular on the sketch comedy series "In Living Color." This exposure led to starring parts in blockbuster films. Carrey's career took off, and he scored parts in smash films such as "Ace Ventura: Pet Detective," "The Mask," and "Dumb and Dumber." By 1995, just before the cheque's expiration date, Carrey had landed a part in "Dumb and Dumber" that earned him a whopping $10 million, the same sum he had put on the check years before. Adding to his stature as a comedy legend.

Carrey's story demonstrates the importance of having objectives, believing in oneself and visualizing one's ambitions until they become a reality. His constant belief in his ability, hard work, and drive enabled him to achieve the success he had always desired.

Important Takeaways

1. Accept failure as a learning experience.
2. When facing hardship, resilience is essential.
3. Even when confronted with skepticism and disappointments, keep moving ahead.
4. Believe in yourself and your abilities to attain your goals.
5. Hard effort and commitment may result in remarkable achievements.

Finally, the inspirational stories of these eighteen amazing people give us essential life lessons. Their stories demonstrate that setbacks and challenges can be overcome with persistence, resilience, and self-belief. We may attain greatness by accepting failure as a stepping stone to achievement and never giving up on our aspirations. So, let these remarkable success stories inspire and drive you as you try to achieve your goals and dreams.

INSPIRATIONAL QUOTES

Everyone needs some inspiration, and these motivational quotations can give you the edge you need to achieve your goals.

Continue reading to discover the words of wisdom that will inspire you to establish your business, lead your life, create success, achieve your goals, and overcome your fears.

1. "Take up one idea. Make that one idea your life--think of it, dream of it, live on that idea. Let the brain, muscles, nerves, every part of your body, be full of that idea, and just leave every other idea alone. This is the way to success." --Swami Vivekananda
2. "If you are not willing to risk the usual you will have to settle for the ordinary." --Jim Rohn
3. "Good things come to people who wait, but better things come to those who go out and get them." --Anonymous
4. . "Whenever you see a successful person you only see the public glories, never the private sacrifices to reach them." --Vaibhav Shah

5. "I have not failed. I've just found 10,000 ways that won't work." --Thomas A. Edison
6. "The meaning of life is to find your gift. The purpose of life is to give it away." --Anonymous
7. "Don't raise your voice, improve your argument." --Anonymous
8. "There are two types of people who will tell you that you cannot make a difference in this world: those who are afraid to try and those who are afraid you will succeed." --Ray Goforth
9. "Success is the sum of small efforts, repeated day-in and day-out." --Robert Collier
10. "Thinking should become your capital asset, no matter whatever ups and downs you come across in your life." --A.P.J. Abdul Kalam
11. . "We become what we think about most of the time, and that's the strangest secret." --Earl Nightingale
12. "People often say that motivation doesn't last. Well, neither does bathing--that's why we recommend it daily." --Zig Ziglar
13. "The road to success and the road to failure are almost exactly the same." --Colin R. Davis
14. "The first step toward success is taken when you refuse to be a captive of the environment in which you first find yourself." --Mark Caine
15. "People who succeed have momentum. The more they succeed, the more they want to succeed, and the more they find a way to succeed. Similarly, when someone is failing, the tendency is to get on a downward spiral

that can even become a self-fulfilling prophecy."
--Tony Robbins

16. "When I dare to be powerful, to use my strength in the service of my vision, then it becomes less and less important whether I am afraid." --Audre Lorde

17. "Develop success from failures. Discouragement and failure are two of the surest stepping stones to success." --Dale Carnegie

18. "If you don't design your own life plan, chances are you'll fall into someone else's plan. And guess what they have planned for you? Not much." --Jim Rohn

19. . "You can't connect the dots looking forward; you can only connect them looking backwards. So you have to trust that the dots will somehow connect in your future. You have to trust in something--your gut, destiny, life, karma, whatever. This approach has never let me down, and it has made all the difference in my life." --Steve Jobs

20. "The reason most people never reach their goals is that they don't define them, or ever seriously consider them as believable or achievable. Winners can tell you where they are going, what they plan to do along the way, and who will be sharing the adventure with them." --Denis Waitley

21. "To be successful you must accept all challenges that come your way. You can't just accept the ones you like." --Mike Gafka

22. "Success is ... knowing your purpose in life, growing to reach your maximum potential, and sowing seeds that benefit others." --John C. Maxwell
23. "A man can be as great as he wants to be. If you believe in yourself and have the courage, the determination, the dedication, the competitive drive and if you are willing to sacrifice the little things in life and pay the price for the things that are worthwhile, it can be done." --Vince Lombardi
24. "Don't let the fear of losing be greater than the excitement of winning." --Robert Kiyosaki
25. "The only limit to our realization of tomorrow will be our doubts of today." - Franklin D. Roosevelt
26. "You are never too old to set another goal or dream a new one." - C.S. Lewis
27. "The only way to do great work is to love what you do." - Steve Jobs
28. "Believe you can, and you're halfway there." - Theodore Roosevelt
29. "The only person you are destined to become is the person you decide to be." - Ralph Waldo Emerson
30. "Your time is limited; don't waste it living someone else's life." - Steve Jobs
31. "You have within you right now everything you need to deal with whatever the world can throw at you." - Brian Tracy
32. "The future belongs to those who believe in the beauty of their dreams." - Eleanor Roosevelt

33. "Success is not final, failure is not fatal: It is the courage to continue that count." - Winston Churchill
34. "Don't watch the clock; do what it does. Keep going."- Sam Levenson
35. "What lies behind us and what lies before us are tiny matters compared to what lies within us." - Ralph Waldo Emerson
36. "The only place where success comes before work is in the dictionary." - Vidal Sassoon
37. "Your attitude, not your aptitude, will determine your altitude." - Zig Ziglar
38. "It always seems impossible until it's done." - Nelson Mandela
39. "Your life does not get better by chance; it gets better by change." - Jim Rohn
40. "The only thing standing between you and your goal is the story you keep telling yourself as to why you can't achieve it." - Jordan Belfort
41. "The only way to achieve the impossible is to believe it is possible." - Charles Kingsleigh (Alice in Wonderland)
42. "The greatest glory in living lies not in never falling, but in rising every time we fall." - Nelson Mandela
43. "The only person who can pull me down is myself, and I'm not going to let myself pull me down anymore." - C. JoyBell C.
44. "You've got to get up every morning with determination if you're going to go to bed with satisfaction." --George Lorimer

As we read these thoughts, remember that they may provide us with advice in times of need, inspiration in times of hardship, and motivation in times of tribulation--success is not final. Failure is not forever; the motivation we select counts most.

AFFIRMATIONS

Reading affirmations cultivates a positive mindset, empowers self-belief, and aligns thoughts with goals, fostering resilience and reducing stress. Here are some affirmations to use:

1. "Embracing each challenge is a step towards my growth, and I welcome the lessons they bring."
2. "In the mirror of self-reflection, I see the strength to overcome any obstacle and the wisdom to turn adversity into opportunity."
3. "My journey is uniquely mine, and I celebrate the progress, no matter how small, knowing it leads to significant transformation."
4. "Every setback is a setup for a greater comeback; I trust in my resilience to turn setbacks into stepping stones."
5. "I release the weight of the past, allowing the present moment to shape a future filled with limitless possibilities."

6. "With each breath, I inhale confidence and exhale self-doubt, paving the way for my empowered journey."
7. "My potential is boundless, and I awaken it with every positive thought and purposeful action."
8. "I am the architect of my destiny, shaping a life that aligns with my deepest passions and aspirations."
9. "Every step I take is a conscious stride towards the extraordinary life I envision for myself."
10. "In the tapestry of my life, I weave threads of gratitude, resilience, and unwavering self-belief."
11. "I radiate positive energy, attracting opportunities that align with my authentic self."
12. "Challenges are invitations to showcase my inner strength, and I embrace them with courage and grace."
13. "My self-worth is non-negotiable, and I honor the unique gifts and talents that make me exceptional."
14. "I release the need for perfection and embrace the beauty of my journey, flaws and all."
15. "With each sunrise, I am reborn, equipped with the power to create a day filled with purpose and joy."
16. "I trust the timing of my life; everything is unfolding in perfect harmony for my highest good."
17. "I am a magnet for positive relationships, drawing in those who uplift and support my journey."
18. "Today, I choose progress over perfection, knowing that small steps lead to significant transformations."
19. "My mind is a garden, and I cultivate thoughts that nurture a flourishing and resilient spirit."

20. "I am a beacon of light, radiating love, compassion, and positivity to everyone I encounter."
21. "I release the need to compare myself to others, acknowledging my unique path and celebrating my achievements."
22. "Every setback is a setup for a comeback, and I rise stronger and more determined each time."
23. "I trust the wisdom of my intuition, guiding me towards choices that align with my authentic self."
24. "I am a vessel of limitless potential, and I unlock my true power with unwavering self-love."
25. "My past does not define me; it provides valuable lessons that propel me towards a brighter future."
26. "I am resilient, resourceful, and ready to embrace the abundance that flows into my life."
27. "I attract prosperity effortlessly, and my financial abundance aligns with my purpose and values."
28. "I release fear and step into the unknown with curiosity, knowing that growth lies beyond my comfort zone."
29. "Every day is an opportunity for a fresh start, and I greet each moment with optimism and enthusiasm."
30. "I am the master of my thoughts, and I choose to focus on what empowers, uplifts, and inspires me."
31. "My mind is a powerhouse of creativity, and I effortlessly channel this creativity into transformative actions."
32. "I release the need for approval from others and validate my worthiness from within."

33. "I am a beacon of resilience, turning challenges into opportunities for personal and spiritual growth."
34. "Every step I take is a dance with destiny, and I am the choreographer of my own success story."
35. "I attract positive energy like a magnet, creating a force field of optimism around me."
36. "I am not a victim of my circumstances; I am the architect of my destiny, shaping a future filled with abundance."
37. "My life is a canvas, and I paint it with the vibrant colors of joy, gratitude, and love."
38. "I trust that the universe conspires in my favor, aligning circumstances for my highest good."
39. "I am a constant work in progress, and I embrace the journey of self-discovery with open arms."
40. "I radiate confidence, and my self-assured presence influences positive outcomes in every situation."
41. "Every challenge is an opportunity to showcase my strength, and I face them with unwavering courage."
42. "I am a magnet for miracles, and I expect the unexpected as I open myself to life's infinite possibilities."
43. "My thoughts create my reality, and I choose thoughts that manifest a life of joy, abundance, and fulfillment."
44. "I am a conduit of love, and I attract relationships that reflect and amplify this boundless love."
45. "I forgive myself for past mistakes and release any lingering guilt, creating space for self-compassion."

46. "I trust in the natural flow of life, surrendering to the journey and allowing it to unfold with grace and ease."
47. "I am a warrior of light, dispelling darkness with the powerful glow of my inner strength and resilience."
48. "I am a vessel of peace, and I carry tranquility within me, radiating it to the world around me."
49. "My potential is limitless, and I dare to dream big, knowing that my dreams are the blueprints of my reality."
50. "I celebrate my uniqueness and express my authentic self boldly, contributing my distinct gifts to the world."
51. "I am a beacon of health and vitality, nurturing my body, mind, and soul with love and respect."
52. "I release attachment to outcomes and trust that the universe is orchestrating the perfect path for me."
53. "I attract abundance in all its forms, recognizing that prosperity flows effortlessly into my life."
54. "I am the captain of my ship, navigating through life's waters with purpose, passion, and a clear vision."
55. "I am a magnet for success, and I attract opportunities that align with my passion and purpose."

CONCLUSION

THE VALUE OF PERSONAL DEVELOPMENT AND SELF-IMPROVEMENT

Individuals who want to live a satisfying and meaningful life must work on themselves and develop personally. It is a path that requires introspection, self-awareness, and the fortitude to face one's flaws. Personal development and self-improvement need continual self-reflection, learning, and skill development. It empowers people to tap into their inner strength, overcome barriers, and realize their full potential. This section will explore the significance of self-improvement and personal development and the advantages it provides to people and society.

Self-improvement and personal progress give people purpose and direction in life. It allows people to discover their strengths, flaws, and places for progress. Individuals may better know their values, beliefs, and ambitions by participating in self-reflection and introspection. Self-aware individuals can better make educated choices, prioritize their time and energy, and connect their activities with their beliefs and goals.

Self-improvement and personal progress can result in increased confidence and self-esteem. Individuals who work on themselves gain new abilities, information, and views to meet new difficulties with increased comfort and confidence.

Individuals may push themselves beyond their boundaries, overcome barriers, and accomplish their goals via personal development and self-improvement. This satisfaction and achievement enhances people's self-esteem and confidence, allowing them to take on bigger tasks and explore new prospects.

Furthermore, self-improvement and personal development add to a person's well-being and happiness. Individuals feel higher levels of enjoyment, contentment, and fulfillment when they engage in activities that encourage personal development, such as gaining new skills, pursuing hobbies, or creating important relationships. These activities give people a feeling of purpose, meaning, and connection, which are important for their psychological and emotional well-being.

Self-improvement and personal progress provide major social advantages in addition to personal rewards. Individuals who pursue personal development and self-improvement are more likely to make meaningful contributions to society. They are likelier to be involved in their communities, seek important occupations, and form strong bonds. Individuals who pursue personal development and self-improvement are also more likely to be empathic, compassionate, and understanding of others. They are more likely to be open-minded, tolerant, and courteous, all necessary for creating cohesive and peaceful societies.

Finally, self-improvement and personal development are crucial for those who want to make a difference. Individuals may become change agents and contribute to the greater good by learning new skills, information, and viewpoints. Personal development and self-improvement empower people to devise novel solutions to complicated issues, question the status quo, and effect good change in their communities and beyond.

In conclusion, self-improvement and personal development are crucial for those who want to live full and meaningful lives. It is a continual process of self-reflection, learning, and skill development that allows people to tap into their inner power, overcome barriers, and realize their full potential. Personal development and self-improvement give people purpose, direction, and confidence, which contributes to their general well-being and pleasure.

ACKNOWLEDGING YOUR PROGRESS AND CELEBRATING YOUR SUCCESSES

Self-improvement is a lifetime endeavor, and it is easy to get overwhelmed by the ongoing drive for progress and change. It is important to realize that growth is not always linear and that setbacks and hurdles are unavoidable. As a result, noting your progress and enjoying your accomplishments are critical components of the self-improvement process.

Recognizing your progress is critical because it gives you perspective and allows you to acknowledge your effort. When we don't take the time to recognize our accomplishments, we risk being locked in a negative attitude, focused only on what we haven't yet done. This might result in emotions of discouragement and demotivation, making it harder to continue on our path to self-improvement.

Begin by reflecting on how far you've come to recognize your progress. Consider the goals you've set for yourself, the challenges you've overcome, and the milestones you've reached. Take the time to record your successes, no matter how little they may seem. This simple gesture of acknowledgment might help you realize your success and give you the courage to keep going.

Celebrating your accomplishments is just as vital as recognizing your progress. Celebrating your accomplishments may give you a feeling of achievement and drive you to keep working toward your goals. Celebrations may be as simple as eating your favorite dish or taking a day off to rest and rejuvenate.

It is important to be focused and thoughtful while celebrating your accomplishments. Avoid underestimating your achievements or feeling guilty for taking time to rejoice. Instead, enjoy the present moment and wallow in your triumph. Remember that celebrating your accomplishments is not only beneficial for your mental health, but it also keeps you motivated and encouraged to keep working toward your goals.

Another method to celebrate your accomplishments is to share them with others. Telling someone about your accomplishments might help you feel appreciated and recognized. It may also motivate others to pursue their ambitions and goals.

However, it is important to be cautious of how you communicate your accomplishments. Avoid coming out as arrogant or boastful. Instead, share your success with humility and thankfulness. Celebrating your accomplishments healthily and pleasantly will help you form stronger relationships with people and build your support network.

Finally, noting your progress and appreciating your accomplishments are critical components of the self-improvement process. Reflecting on your achievements and celebrating your victories may help you remain motivated, inspire others, and strengthen your relationships. Remember to be purposeful and thoughtful while celebrating your victories, and avoid downplaying your achievements or feeling guilty. With this technique, you may attain your goals while still having fun on your road to personal development and self-improvement.

The notion of a growth mindset is becoming more prevalent in self-improvement and personal progress. Carol Dweck, a psychology professor at Stanford University, coined the phrase "growth mindset" in her book "Mindset: The New Psychology of Success." According to Dweck, individuals with a growth mindset think that their talents and intellect can be enhanced through devotion and hard effort. Rather than being a setback or a reflection of their innate talents, they perceive failure as a chance for development and learning.

Individuals with a fixed mentality, on the other hand, feel that their talents and intellect are fixed and cannot be altered. They may shun challenges or risks out of fear of failure, and when confronted with failures, they may feel disappointed or rejected.

The good news is that, with practice and determination, a growth mindset can be nurtured and developed over time. Here are some pointers for adopting a development mindset and accepting good change:

Recognize and question limiting beliefs

Limiting beliefs are negative or self-defeating ideas that might prevent us from reaching our goals. They may result from prior events, cultural messaging, or our self-talk. Limiting beliefs might include things like "I'm not smart enough," "I don't have enough experience," or "I'll never be able to do it."

Recognizing and challenging limiting ideas is the first step in overcoming them. "Is this belief based on facts or assumptions?" you should ask yourself.

"Am I considering all of my strengths and experiences?" Reframe your self-talk to emphasize possibilities and progress rather than limitation and defeat.

Accept failures and learn from your mistakes

On the route to success and progress, challenges and failures are unavoidable. Instead of avoiding them, see them as chances for learning and progress. Remember that failure is not a reflection of your value or intellect but a necessary element of the learning process.

When confronted with a difficulty or failure, ask yourself, "What can I learn from this experience?" "How can I use this feedback to make future improvements?" Reframe failure as a stepping stone to success, not a hindrance or a reflection on your talents.

Practiced Self-compassion and kindness

Self-compassion is treating oneself with the same love, care, and understanding that one would provide to a good friend. It entails identifying and embracing your shortcomings and defects while appreciating your talents and successes.

Self-compassion may aid in developing a growth mindset by instilling a feeling of self-worth and resilience. When confronted with a setback or failure, treat yourself with care and compassion instead of self-criticism or blame. Remember that everyone makes errors and that learning and growing requires time and effort.

Surround yourself with positive people

The individuals we associate with greatly influence our mentality and conduct. Instead of individuals who pull you down or discourage you, surround yourself with positive influences that uplift and motivate you. Seek mentors, coaches, or peers who share your beliefs and goals and may provide encouragement and support.

Set realistic goals and track your progress

Goal setting is a crucial component of the growth mindset process. Goals help us concentrate and track progress while offering direction and purpose. However, it is critical to create reasonable and attainable goals rather than ambitious or unrealistic ones that may lead to failure.

Break your goals into smaller, more doable tasks, and keep track of your progress. Celebrate your victories, seeing setbacks and obstacles as chances for learning and progress.